THE COOKIN' CAJUN
COOKING SCHOOL COOKBOOK

Lisette Verlander ❖ Susan Murphy

GIBBS-SMITH
➔P
PUBLISHER

SALT LAKE CITY

4.3.99

To Tomoko,
Enjoy This
Great Taste of
Louisiana!
Susan Murphy

99 98 97   5 4 3 2

This is a Peregrine Smith Book, published by
Gibbs Smith, Publisher
P.O. Box 667
Layton, Utah 84041

Cover illustration by Martha Guthrie
Interior illustrations by Martha Guthrie, Susan Ross Evans
Design by Leesha Jones
Edited by Caroll Shreeve with contributing editors Mary Kelly and Jennifer Howard

Printed in Hong Kong

LIBRARY OF CONGRESS CATALOGING-IN-PUBLICATION DATA

Verlander, Lisette, 1928-
    The Cookin' Cajun Cooking School cookbook. / Lisette Verlander, Susan Murphy
    p. cm.
    Includes index.
    ISBN 0-87905-784-X
    1. Cookery, Cajun.   2. Cookery, American—Louisiana style.
I Murphy, Susan, 1945-   . II. Title.
TX715.2.L68V47 1997
641.59763—dc20   96-33612
                                                              CIP

CONTENTS

FRONT AND BACK INSIDE COVERS:
YOUR CAJUN/CREOLE DELICACIES
    SHOPPING LIST (A-Z)

DEDICATION

I will always remember meeting Lee Barnes for the first time. Lee had a cooking school in uptown New Orleans, and I had decided to take a course in microwave cooking there. My husband had just given me my first microwave oven, and I had no idea what to do with it other than heat leftovers.

Lee had brought in an expert in the field of microwave cooking to give the class, but I remember Lee was always there to assist the instructor. She was calm and professional but also added a touch of humor to the class with an occasional funny remark. Many of my friends took classes with her, and we all had wonderful experiences.

It wasn't until years later that I met Lee again when she came with Susan Murphy for an interview about helping us open Cookin' Cajun Cooking School. We knew immediately that they would be easy and fun to work with, as well as perfect for the job.

Lee had attended the Cordon Bleu cooking school in Paris and had owned and operated her own cooking school for many years. Lee's motto was, "Love to eat? Learn to cook!"

Students always loved her classes. In almost all our classes, we use the recipes she developed and have included them in this cookbook.

Lee died from a brain tumor in November 1993; we were all devastated. She was only forty-two. We will remember her warmth and humor. We owe her so much for making our cooking school the success it is today, and also for being a good friend.

A special culinary scholarship has been established in Lee's honor. A portion of all sales of this cookbook in our store or by Creole Delicacies mail order will go toward this worthy cause.

It is in Lee's honor that we dedicate this cookbook.

LISETTE VERLANDER SUTTON

Foreword

As a young boy growing up in New Orleans, I learned a lot from my mother's kitchen. I learned to love the tastes and smells of good food, and that true Southern hospitality begins in the kitchen, the soul of a home.

The Verlanders invite people into their kitchen daily to offer what is best about New Orleans—real food and great people coming together to make a memory. They have created a place overlooking the mighty Mississippi River where visitors as well as locals can gather to learn what is so special about this area's fresh produce, the cultures from which many of the recipes originate, and the traditions that make our food so memorable.

People travel from all over the world to sample such delights as gumbos, étouffées, jambalayas, and rémoulades that may include crawfish, shrimp, oysters, tasso, boudins, or fish. They come with family and friends to share in the fun. And now, they can take these experiences and recreate them in their own kitchens.

My family and the Verlanders have been friends for three generations. Our families have a common dream, the dream of sharing a love of our home and all that it represents with those interested in listening. I remember, well, the youngest Verlander knocking on my door with pralines for us to sample. These small beginnings, driven by tremendous energy, have made it possible for all to learn the excitement and magic of creating delicious foods and fun times in their own kitchens, very similar to that of my mother, I'm sure.

Today, the Verlanders' business has grown and evolved just as Creole and Cajun cooking have evolved. Yet, one thing remains constant—the roots from which they have grown. This family—through Cookin' Cajun Cooking School, Creole Delicacies, and now this book—share their heritage, their love of a great city, and their tremendous passion for good food and good times.

Dick Brennan
Owner/Managing Partner
Commander's Palace Restaurant
New Orleans, Louisiana

Welcome to Cookin' Cajun

Two of the world's most popular regional cuisines, Cajun and Creole, blend the flavors of fresh ingredients with New Orleans' rich French, Spanish, and Caribbean heritage. The result is a jazzy, robust taste that enhances even the most everyday ingredients.

We are frequently asked at Cookin' Cajun Cooking School, "What's the difference between Cajun and Creole cooking?" Creole cooking requires more seasonings and oils, which make its flavor intense. The dishes are rich in texture and often begin with a roux, a browned mixture of flour and oil. Most Creole dishes reflect the sophistication of Louisiana's cities and their lively social styles.

Cajun dishes are Creole's country cousins. Developed by the descendants of French-speaking Acadians banished from Nova Scotia in the 1700s, Cajun cuisine features dishes using simple ingredients that can generally be prepared in one large pot.

The rich culinary heritage and traditions that have created this area's outstanding cuisine are a lot like the ingredients for gumbo, a traditional Cajun soup so rich and hearty that it's almost a stew. The area's natural advantages—its abundant seafood from local waters and ample regionally grown produce—are like the roux that is the basis of a good gumbo. The roux gives the gumbo its character, and New Orleans' plentiful fresh seafood and access to seasonal vegetables determine the basic character of Creole and Cajun cooking.

There are many kinds of gumbo, because thrifty Cajun and Creole housewives wasted little and worked almost anything into a tasty gumbo. Culinary professionals as well as gifted home chefs who took the foods available locally and created unique dishes are a metaphor for the seafood, fowl, and assorted vegetables in a gumbo. All have contributed to the rich stew that has become the essence of Creole and Cajun cuisine.

A gumbo that doesn't have a zesty, spicy flavor is not a gumbo at all. Adding the zip and zing to New Orleans cuisine is the city's propensity to party. The City That Care Forgot celebrates more events and holidays than any other place on earth. To a Cajun or Creole, if there's no excuse to party, getting together with friends still calls for good food.

At Cookin' Cajun Cooking School, we enjoy sharing our rich culinary heritage through a range of classes that focus on delicious recipes, techniques and good times.

In our Creole Delicacies gourmet shop adjoining the cooking school, you'll find the best of Louisiana spices, hot sauces, ingredients, and kitchen equipment. Some of the locally produced items may be difficult to find outside the area, so we offer our guests the opportunity to purchase them after cooking classes. We prepare many of the mixes, sauces, and spices ourselves in our Creole Delicacies Kitchens, and we recommend them highly.

With this book, you'll be able to bring Cajun and Creole cuisine right into your own kitchen. We've included both traditional and more up-to-date recipes, as well as all the tips, techniques, and ingredient information you'll need. We have shared the spirit of the city that has captured the imaginations of so many great chefs. We hope you will find yourself inspired and delighted with the tantalizing dishes you'll be creating.

IT'S A FAMILY AFFAIR

We are real New Orleans people, born and raised here for several generations. It was only natural that our family took our interest in food one step further, establishing Cookin' Cajun Cooking School and its parent company, Creole Delicacies. We enjoy life and we especially enjoy great food.

My youngest brother, Tim, had just left home for college at the University of Alabama when our family bought a small business on St. Ann Street in the French Quarter called Creole Delicacies. Mom, otherwise known as Big Lisette, joined my brother Ken and me in our first venture into the gourmet food business. We couldn't have done it without the help of Geraldine Burras Gooseberry, the greatest praline maker of all time, who presided over our kitchen. Now, Mom concentrates on our catalog and mail-order business, which has grown every year.

Note that this Creole Delicacies logo is a cue throughout the recipes for Cajun ingredients available by mail order.

As our business grew from one shop to several, we had more and more requests to sell our food products wholesale. Our brothers Harry and Tim joined us to open the Creole Delicacies Kitchens in Metairie, where we make our creamy pralines, as well as our whole line of Creole Delicacies and Cookin' Cajun products—including our popular Mardi Gras Dip.

We had long wanted to share our knowledge and love of this very special cuisine in our area, and opening Cookin' Cajun Cooking School in 1988 was the best decision we ever made. We were so lucky to find the perfect people to help us organize and run our fledgling school—Lee Barnes and Susan Murphy. Students loved their classes and delicious recipes and still do.

Cookin' Cajun Cooking School is open year-round, offering daily classes. Our Riverwalk Marketplace location in the very heart of downtown New Orleans, across Canal Street from the French Quarter, provides a magnificent view of the Mississippi River. We invite you to join our family soon at Cookin' Cajun to discover the fun and flavors of cooking Louisiana style.

BON APPETIT!
LISETTE VERLANDER SUTTON

CELEBRATIONS AND LIBATIONS

Laissez les bons temps rouler—or "let the good times roll"—is the closest thing New Orleans has to a citywide motto. In "the city that care forgot," the Creole and Cajun traditional calendar of celebrations and parties is an impressive year-round chronicle of events that bring together family and friends to enjoy the good times—as well as delicious foods and beverages. Partying in South Louisiana begins at Thanksgiving, followed by holiday parties that lead to Christmas, and on to New Year's and the Sugar Bowl festivities.

On Twelfth Night, January 6, the celebratory countdown to Mardi Gras begins. King cakes—large, doughnut-shaped sweet breads decorated with the traditional Carnival colors of green (faith), purple (justice), and gold (power) appear. In each cake, a small plastic doll is hidden. The person who receives it must give the next king cake party, a cycle that runs from year to year.

Mardi Gras balls—lavish, formal dances given by Carnival krewes—begin just after New Year's with private dinners given by krewe members, and ends with a fortifying breakfast just before dawn.

The traditional forty-day Lenten season leading to Easter calls for family gatherings and an array of seasonal cuisine. At Easter, the festival season kicks in. Cajuns can make a festive event out of celebrating almost anything—from the lowly crawfish to the annual blessing of the town's fishing fleet, plus graduations and weddings.

Summer is hot in South Louisiana, but Cajuns and Creoles beat the heat by taking the cooking outdoors. Many homes have a second, outdoor kitchen used for barbecuing and shrimp or crawfish boils, with most of the food cooked in one huge boiling pot.

With autumn's cooler weather, football season calls for more parties. Halloween is primarily for children, but October 31 includes visits to the grave of Marie Laveau, the voodoo queen. New Orleans resident Anne Rice's vampire novels have spawned spooky adult parties. After Halloween and All Saints Day (November 1), the cycle begins again.

The word "cocktail" was first coined in the late 1700s, when Antoine Amdee Peychaud developed a tonic he called "bitters" in his apothecary shop in the French Quarter. He served this tonic with cognac in a section of an egg cup, known in French as a *coquetier*. Americans mispronounced the word, and the potion and others similar to it became known as a "cocktail."

But you don't have to drink alcohol to enjoy the good times. In New Orleans, it is always in good taste to order a cup of steaming café au lait or a Barq's root beer.

HURRICANE

One of New Orleans' most famous drinks, it is said to be named after the killer storms, because you never know when it's going to hit you; and after a few too many, you feel like a hurricane blew through your head. Created by the famous Pat O'Brien's, this drink is a favorite among visitors to the Crescent City.

4 ounces (¹/₂ cup) dark rum
4 ounces (¹/₂ cup) Pat O'Brien's ™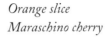
   Hurricane Mix

Orange slice
Maraschino cherry

1. Combine rum and Hurricane Mix. Serve in a Hurricane glass filled with crushed ice. Garnish with orange slice and cherry. Serves 1.

RAMOS GIN FIZZ

"This is delicious" is the first thing most people say after tasting their first Ramos Gin Fizz. "Is there alcohol in it?" This drink was created in New Orleans over 100 years ago by Henry Ramos.

1 teaspoon lemon or lime juice
2 teaspoons powdered sugar
3 drops orange flower water
1 drop vanilla extract

2 ounces (¹/₄ cup) gin
2 ounces (¹/₄ cup) cream
1 cup cracked ice
Orange slice

Optional: 1 egg white, beaten. Most of today's recipes have eliminated the raw egg white because of possible health hazard. Pasteurized eggs are available in some locations.

1. In a cocktail shaker or container with lid, combine all ingredients and shake thoroughly for several minutes. Strain into a tall chilled glass. Serves 1.

CAJUN MIMOSA

This drink is *gar-on-teed* to spice up any brunch! We prefer to use fresh juice of low-acid oranges, which is also available in frozen concentrate.

1 quart orange juice
1 magnum chilled champagne

Crushed ice

1. Fill tall, stemmed glasses halfway with crushed ice. Fill with half orange juice and then half champagne. Stir gently before serving. Serves 8.

For a Cajun touch, add 3 drops Tabasco Jalapeño Sauce before serving.

NEW ORLEANS MINT JULEP

When thinking of Southern beverages, the Mint Julep comes almost immediately to mind. Although it did not originate in New Orleans, this cooling drink was soon brought to the city. Elegant in its simplicity, a Mint Julep is still good company on a hot, humid afternoon. It is best served in a traditional silver tumbler that has been chilled in the refrigerator for a few hours.

5 mint leaves plus one sprig for garnish
1 teaspoon confectioner's sugar
1 teaspoon water

1½ ounces (2½ tablespoons) bourbon whiskey
Crushed ice

1. Stir mint leaves, sugar, and water until sugar is dissolved. Add bourbon. Pour over crushed ice. Garnish with mint sprig. Serves 1.

MILK PUNCH

Another "morning after" remedy, this rich, sweet, and velvety punch is popular at jazz brunches.

1¹/₂ ounces bourbon whiskey
(or brandy, if you prefer)
2 ounces (¹/₄ cup) milk
1 ounce (2 tablespoons) cream
(or half-and-half or coffee creamer)

¹/₂ teaspoon sugar
2 drops vanilla
4 ice cubes
Fresh ground nutmeg

1. Stir or shake together all ingredients except nutmeg. Pour into a tall glass, straining out the ice cubes. Garnish with a sprinkle of nutmeg. Serves 1.

NEW ORLEANS OLD-FASHIONED

In New Orleans, this popular drink was made with rye whiskey in the old days, but now, most prefer to use bourbon whiskey. We have a wonderful Higgins Old-Fashioned Mix available in our shop or by mail order.

1 teaspoon sugar
1 tablespoon water
2 to 3 dashes Angostura Bitters
1 twist lemon peel
2 ounces (¹/₄ cup) rye or bourbon whiskey

Ice cubes
1 ounce (2 tablespoons) club soda
Maraschino cherry
¹/₂ slice orange

1. Dissolve sugar in water in a double Old-Fashioned glass. Add bitters, lemon peel, and rye or bourbon. Add ice cubes and top off with club soda. Garnish with cherry and orange slice. Serves 1.

CHICORY DEFINES NEW ORLEANS COFFEE

New Orleanians love their coffee. We love our café au lait in which milk dilutes the strong coffee.

Most coffee you'll be served in New Orleans contains chicory, the finely ground root of the endive plant. It may seem strange to add a vegetable to coffee, but the practice came to New Orleans from France where it was done out of necessity during the Napoleonic era. The French had come to love coffee, and when a naval blockade denied them their supply, they tried to substitute barley. The resulting drink was so bland that full-bodied, peppery chicory was added to pep it up.

Even after the fall of Napoleon, the thrifty French continued adding chicory to their coffee to stretch it. The practice was brought to New Orleans, where it became part of the culture.

Authentic New Orleans coffee is dark roasted and blended with 30 percent and 40 percent chicory. It's served strong and hot.

CAFÉ BRÛLOT

The perfect ending to a festive meal.

2 cinnamon sticks
3 tablespoons sugar
6 whole cloves
4 ounces brandy

1 ounce curaçao
Zest of one lemon
4 cups hot New Orleans Coffee and Chicory
  (dark roast)

1. Scrape the zest (peel) from the lemon, using a lemon zester. Heat all ingredients except coffee until hot but not boiling.

2. Pour into silver brûlot bowl or chafing dish over heat source, and ignite. Add the very hot coffee and stir gently. Use a long-handled ladle to serve in demitasse cups or tall narrow brûlot cups. Serves 4.

Café au Lait

New Orleans natives enjoy their Café au Lait (coffee with milk) from breakfast to bedtime.

1 cup boiling milk (skim milk may be used)
1 cup hot New Orleans Coffee and Chicory
   (dark roast)

Sugar to taste

1. Pour boiling milk and hot coffee at same time into your favorite coffee cup. Sweeten to taste. Serves 2.

The leftover mixture makes delicious iced coffee!

Irish Coffee

New Orleanians love coffee, so no one knows if the nineteenth-century influx of Irish to the city brought along Irish Coffee or if it arrived on its own.

1 ounce (2 tablespoons) Irish whiskey
1 teaspoon sugar

Hot New Orleans Coffee and Chicory (dark roast)
Whipped cream

1. Mix Irish whiskey and sugar in an eight-ounce stemmed glass or coffee mug until sugar is dissolved. Fill glass within an inch or so of the top with hot coffee. Top with whipped cream. Serves 1.

STARBOARD LIGHT

Dad has taught bartenders across the country to make Starboard Lights and their opposite, Port Lights.

1 ounce (2 tablespoons) vodka or gin
1 ounce (2 tablespoons) green crème de menthe

Crushed ice

1. Mix ingredients and serve in a short glass over ice. Serves 1.

PORT LIGHT

1 ounce (2 tablespoons) vodka or gin
1 ounce (2 tablespoons) white crème de menthe

Few drops red food coloring
Crushed ice

1. Mix ingredients and serve over ice in a short glass. Serves 1.

BLOODY MARY

There are a host of options when you make this drink—you can serve the one that best fits the occasion and your mood.

2 ounces (¹/₄ cup) vodka (a bar brand)
2 ounces (¹/₄ cup) V8 Juice
1 ounce Jero's Bloody Mary Mix (or your favorite
  brand)

Dash celery salt (or plain salt)
Dash finely ground black pepper
Dash Worcestershire sauce
Dash hot sauce

1. Put all ingredients into a ten-ounce glass with ice cubes. Stir well. Garnish with a wedge of lemon or lime and a small sprig of celery or a pickled green bean. Serves 1.

SPECIAL OPTIONS:
  a. Add ¹/₂ teaspoon prepared horseradish. Stir well.
  b. Add one ounce beer, from a bar tap if available. It gives an incredible boost to the flavor.

BLOODY MARYS FOR A PARTY

(1) 1-liter bottle vodka
(1) 750-milliliter bottle Bloody Mary mix
  (Jero's or use your favorite brand)
(1) 48-ounce can V8 Juice
1 can beef bouillon

Juice of 3 lemons
1 tablespoon salt
1 tablespoon finely ground black pepper
1 tablespoon Tabasco
2 tablespoons Worcestershire sauce

1. Mix all ingredients in large stockpot or other container. When well mixed, transfer to attractive glass pitchers to place on the bar. Serve in eight- or ten-ounce glasses over ice cubes. Garnish with a wedge of lemon or lime and a small sprig of celery. Yield: 32 drinks, four ounces each.

Appetizing Beginnings

People say that New Orleanians never meet or have an event without delicious food. In the Crescent City, good food is part of having a good time. Appetizers do double duty as first courses at dinner or as finger food at parties and other events.

Cajun and Creole cuisines offer a host of sauces and dips that add extra zip to more traditional appetizers, such as raw vegetables or chips. We've included recipes for appetizers that are uniquely representative of Louisiana's culinary heritage. Enjoy!

Quick Shrimp Newburg

This recipe is a good way to use leftover boiled shrimp. Created by Lee Barnes.

2 cups cooked, peeled shrimp
3 tablespoons butter
1 bunch green onions, chopped
3 tablespoons flour
1/2 teaspoon Creole Mustard
1/4 teaspoon black pepper

1 teaspoon salt
1 cup evaporated milk
    (skim can be used successfully)
1 1/2 cups water
2 tablespoons sherry

1. Cut shrimp in half lengthwise. Melt butter in a saucepan over very low heat, and sauté the green onions until tender. Incorporate the flour until well blended, add the seasonings, and mix well.

2. Remove the pan from the heat, and slowly stir in evaporated milk and water. Cook over medium heat until the mixture thickens.

3. Remove from heat and add the sherry, followed by the shrimp. Heat thoroughly; serve immediately. Serves 7 or 8.

OYSTERS IBERVILLE

Iberville was the brother of Bienville, the founder of New Orleans. Both French brothers are said to have enjoyed the oysters they discovered in the bayous near the mouth of the Mississippi River. Oysters Iberville is delicious served over buttered toast. Created by Lee Barnes.

1 pound shrimp
¼ pound (1 stick) unsalted butter
1 bunch shallots (green onions), finely chopped
½ teaspoon salt
Black pepper
½ cup chicken or seafood consommé

1½ cups white wine
2 dozen oysters, pre-shucked in jars with liquor
Tabasco or other hot-pepper sauce to taste
Seasoned bread crumbs
Melted butter

1. Peel and finely chop the shrimp. Melt butter in a saucepan and add the shallots. Sauté for a couple of minutes; then add the chopped shrimp, the salt, and a sprinkle of black pepper. Cook while stirring for five minutes.

2. In another saucepan, pour the consommé and white wine together, and bring to a boil. Add the oysters and their liquid. Cook until the edges of the oysters begin to curl. Add a few drops of Tabasco or other hot-pepper sauce.

3. Place the oysters in the bottom of a casserole and place shrimp on top. Sprinkle liberally with seasoned bread crumbs that have been mixed with melted butter. Place casserole dish under a broiler. When the crumbs are brown (two to three minutes), the dish is ready to serve. Serves 6 to 8.

OYSTER PATTIES

These bite-sized appetizers are wedding staples in New Orleans. The rich oyster filling is also delicious served over toast. This is another of Lee Barnes' favorites.

1 bunch green onions, chopped
2 cloves garlic, minced
3 tablespoons butter
2 heaping tablespoons flour

$2^{1}/_{2}$ dozen oysters, pre-shucked in jars with liquor
1 pint light cream
$^{1}/_{2}$ bunch Italian parsley, chopped
Bite-sized patty shells

1. Sauté onions and garlic in butter until tender. Add flour to make a white roux, being careful not to brown it.

2. Bring oysters to a boil in their own liquor. Drain and check for any grit. Chop oysters. Slowly stir the oyster liquor into the roux. Add cream, then parsley. Simmer about 15 minutes. Season to taste.

3. Add oysters three minutes before serving. Spoon into patty shells or over toast and serve warm. Serves 6 to 8.

❖

OYSTERS IN LIQUOR
Creole cooks have long known that much of the oyster flavor is imparted to a dish by the water or "liquor" in jars with shucked oysters. You'll find that most Creole and Cajun recipes use this liquid as well as the oysters. Some cooks with families or friends who don't like a heavier oyster flavor will substitute broth or consommé.

SPICY FRIED EGGPLANT FINGERS

Delicious Fried Eggplant Fingers remain one of our most popular dishes. Try this recipe with other vegetables, but do not salt them as you would ordinarily prepare eggplant. Other vegetables that work well are yellow squash, zucchini, mushrooms, green tomatoes, steamed broccoli, cauliflower, and okra. This recipe is a good way to get people who refuse to eat most vegetables to eat the recommended daily requirement. You can also use frozen cheese.

We recommend peanut or canola oil for frying; both tolerate the high heat necessary for deep-frying without breaking down and smoking. The Eggplant Fingers freeze well. Batter them, but don't cook them before freezing. They will hold up for 3 to 4 days.

Salt	*1 to 2 cups flour*
1 eggplant, cut in finger–long strips	*¼ teaspoon black pepper*
2 eggs	*¼ teaspoon white pepper*
1 cup milk	*Italian bread crumbs*
Tabasco or other hot-pepper sauce to taste	*Oil for frying*

1. Salt eggplant fingers and allow to drain in a colander for 20 minutes. Rinse and dry well. Do not salt the other vegetables.

2. Combine eggs, milk, and Tabasco. Dip the eggplant fingers into flour seasoned with pepper, then into egg mixture, followed by bread crumbs. Deep-fry until golden brown.

3. A small eggplant will serve three; a large one will serve five. Figure three fingers per person. Serve with dip, such as our famous Cookin' Cajun Mardi Gras Dip.

Olive Nut Dip

A spicy, salty treat your guests will love. Try this in stuffed celery, too.

8 ounces cream cheese, softened
$^1/_2$ cup mayonnaise
$^1/_2$ cup chopped pecans

1 cup salad olives, chopped
2 tablespoons olive juice
Cayenne pepper to taste

1. Mix all ingredients well. Chill for 24 hours. Serve with your favorite snack crackers or raw vegetables. Serves 10 to 12.

Cajun Cheese Ball

This recipe is just the right size to serve a few guests. Double it or triple it for a crowd.

8 ounces cream cheese
3 tablespoons minced onion
4 ounces grated cheddar cheese
1 ounce blue or Roquefort cheese, crumbled

Dash of Worcestershire sauce
$^1/_4$ teaspoon cayenne pepper
2 tablespoons parsley, finely chopped
$^1/_2$ cup pecans, finely chopped

1. Combine first six ingredients. Soften in microwave for one minute. Mix well and shape into a ball or log.

2. Mix parsley and pecans together. Roll cheese ball in pecan mix until completely covered. Chill. Serve with crackers. Serves 12.

TRADITIONAL RÉMOULADE SAUCE

This is a very versatile sauce. Traditionally served on boiled shrimp on top of shredded lettuce, it's also delicious on sliced tomatoes, as a dressing for pasta salad, or in chicken or potato salad. For delightfully different deviled eggs, mix Rémoulade Sauce with mayonnaise.

The sauce doubles easily, and will last five to seven days in the refrigerator.

1 medium onion
1 bunch green onions
1 stalk celery
2 cloves garlic
¼ cup parsley
1 tablespoon paprika
¼ teaspoon cayenne pepper

2 teaspoons salt
½ cup Creole Mustard
2 tablespoons lemon juice
2 tablespoons vinegar
1 tablespoon Worcestershire sauce
4 shakes Tabasco or other hot-pepper sauce
¾ cup oil

1. Combine all ingredients except oil in food processor. Turn on and slowly dribble in oil until smooth. Refrigerate. Allow flavors to marry for up to 24 hours, or at least 20 minutes. Season to taste.

WHITE RÉMOULADE SAUCE

We learned to love this sauce at Pascal's Manale Restaurant in uptown New Orleans. They served a combination dish of shrimp and lump crabmeat over shredded lettuce, topped with White Rémoulade Sauce over half the serving and red cocktail sauce over the other half. It is outstanding!

1 cup mayonnaise
¼ cup Creole Mustard

1 teaspoon fresh lemon juice

1. Mix all ingredients. Chill. Serve over boiled shrimp or crabmeat, or use as a dip for shrimp or crab claws.

ROCKEFELLER SAUCE

This incredible sauce was created at Antoine's Restaurant. When it was invented, Rockefeller was the richest man in America—which tells you something about the delicious richness this sauce brings to a dish.

Rockefeller Sauce is very versatile. Serve as a dip with garlic rounds or plain crackers. It enhances chicken breasts, pasta, or veal. For pasta, thin the sauce with ½ cup of the water used for boiling the pasta, wine, milk, half-and-half, or cream. Toss the thinned sauce with pasta, and serve with fried oysters on the side. Lasagna made by building layers with Rockefeller Sauce is a unique treat. Use this sauce to dress up baked, broiled, smoked, or fried fish. For a garnish or to accompany an entrée, try it as a stuffing for mushroom caps.

4 tablespoons unsalted butter
2 stalks celery, chopped
6 green onions, chopped
1 bunch Italian parsley, chopped
(1) 10-ounce package frozen spinach, cooked and
    drained, squeezed dry

1 tablespoon anchovy paste
1 tablespoon ketchup
¼ cup Herbsaint or Pernod
Pepper (black, white, or a combination) to taste
Tabasco or other hot-pepper sauce to taste
¼ pound (1 stick) unsalted butter, softened

1. Melt butter. Sauté celery, green onions, and parsley until tender. Add spinach. Place ingredients in a food processor and purée.

2. Add anchovy paste, ketchup, Herbsaint, and black or white pepper. Season to taste with Tabasco. Add remaining stick of butter and purée. Rockefeller Sauce doubles or triples quantities easily and freezes beautifully.

At Cookin' Cajun, we slice French bread about ⅓-inch thick, and then toast it until it is hard and dry. Place a poached oyster on the bread. Cover the oyster and bread completely with Rockefeller Sauce and broil until hot and bubbly for a heavenly party finger food.

If you don't enjoy or can't buy fresh oysters, sauté fresh, sliced mushrooms. Top the bread with the mushrooms, cover with Rockefeller Sauce, and broil. Covers about 12 to 15 rounds of bread.

SHRIMP BEIGNETS

Beignets, the traditional Creole doughnuts, are not just for breakfast or served with Café au Lait anymore. We've created a delicious recipe using puffy fried beignets with shrimp and spices that makes a wonderful appetizer. Clams, smoked chicken, crawfish, mushrooms, and crabmeat are delicious shrimp alternatives in Creole beignets.

2 cups flour
2 tablespoons baking powder
$1/2$ teaspoon ground ginger
$1/4$ cup pimentos, diced and drained
1 tablespoon garlic, chopped
$1^1/2$ cups cooked shrimp

3 green onions, chopped
3 tablespoons plain parsley, chopped
3 dashes hot-pepper sauce
$1^1/2$ cups water
Canola or peanut oil

1. Mix dry ingredients together evenly. Add all other ingredients except water and hot sauce. Mix well.

2. Add water and hot sauce, but just enough to form a loose dough. Set aside for 15 minutes to rest.

3. Preheat canola or peanut oil in fryer to 350°F. Spoon in dough by the teaspoon. Deep fry until golden brown.

4. Remove from oil and drain on paper towels. Serve with tartar sauce or Mardi Gras Dip. Yield: 30 beignets. Serves 10 with 3 each.

CRAWFISH DIP

Serve this richly flavored dip—hot—with corn chips, pretzels, or snack crackers to spice up any party.

1 onion, chopped
1 bell pepper, chopped
2 ribs celery, chopped
1/2 cup parsley, chopped
1 stick margarine
1 tablespoon flour

2 cans cream of mushroom soup
1 pound crawfish tails
1/4 cup ketchup
1 teaspoon light Worcestershire sauce
1 teaspoon hot-pepper sauce (or to taste)

1. Sauté onion, bell pepper, celery, and parsley in margarine until well cooked and almost browned. Add flour, and stir well.

2. Add soup and crawfish. Simmer 30 minutes. Add ketchup, light Worcestershire sauce, and hot-pepper sauce. Mix well and serve immediately. Serves 12.

SHRIMP DIP

Charlotte Stead, our most organized staff member, also prepares her scrumptious Shrimp Dip. Although it easily serves 12 people, five or six of us have been known to finish an entire bowl at one sitting.

(1) 8-ounce package cream cheese
(1) 6-ounce can shrimp
$\frac{1}{2}$ onion, finely chopped
1 teaspoon lemon juice

2 teaspoons Worcestershire sauce
$\frac{1}{4}$ teaspoon Tabasco or other hot-pepper sauce
1 to 2 tablespoons evaporated milk

1. Soften cream cheese. Drain shrimp and crumble them into the cream cheese. Add onion, lemon juice, Worcestershire sauce, Tabasco, and evaporated milk. Mix well. Serve with crackers. Serves 12.

It's Soup!

Cajun and Creole chefs often cooked for a crowd, whether for their families or for a party. They were thrifty cooks who knew how to stretch food in delicious ways, accomplishing the challenge by preparing soup, a skill that Cajun and Creole chefs have developed to an art.

Although gumbo is perhaps the best known soup from South Louisiana chefs' recipe boxes, there are other delicious soups that are just as tasty. Many are traditional soups that use seafood, game, and locally available vegetables. Here are the Cookin' Cajun Cooking School favorites.

Gumbo Z'Herbes

This unusual gumbo features green vegetables and oysters where more traditional gumbos use seafood and okra or chicken and sausage. Serve with hot corn bread. Gumbo Z'Herbes may look difficult to make, but it isn't. It will warm the soul on a cold night. This recipe calls for frozen vegetables, but fresh ones can be used. Wash one bunch of each variety well, and remove the stems.

2 quarts water or chicken stock
(1) 10-ounce package frozen spinach
(1) 10-ounce package frozen mustard greens
(1) 10-ounce package frozen turnip greens
(1) 10-ounce package frozen collard greens
$^1/_2$ medium cabbage, shredded
4 bay leaves
1 teaspoon basil
1 teaspoon thyme
$^1/_8$ teaspoon allspice

$^1/_8$ teaspoon cloves
$^1/_4$ pound (1 stick) butter, divided in half
2 onions, chopped
1 cup bell pepper, chopped
1 cup celery, chopped
2 tablespoons oil
1 pound beef stew meat, cut into small pieces
    (optional)
1 slice ham, cut into pieces (optional)
1 bunch green onions, chopped

Gumbo Z'Herbes (cont'd)

½ cup parsley, chopped
4 cloves garlic, chopped
1 dozen oysters with liquor
Tabasco or other hot-pepper sauce to taste

Salt and black pepper to taste
5 tablespoons flour
Hot cooked rice

1. To the water or stock, add spinach, mustard greens, turnip greens, collard greens, cabbage, bay leaves, basil, thyme, allspice, and cloves. Bring to a boil. Lower heat and let simmer, covered.

2. In a frying pan, sauté half stick of the butter with the onions, bell pepper, and celery. When vegetables are browned, add to the pot with the greens.

3. In the same frying pan, add oil, stew meat, and ham. When browned, add to the pot.

4. Add the green onions, parsley, and garlic. Add Tabasco or hot-pepper sauce, salt, and pepper to taste. Simmer covered for at least two hours.

5. After simmering for an hour, work the remaining butter into a paste with flour. When the paste is smooth, slice a bit of it at a time into the big pot. Don't be alarmed if it looks lumpy. The lumps will disappear as you stir. Five minutes before serving, add the oysters and their liquid. Cook till the edges of the oysters curl. Serve over rice. Serves 12.

❖

GUMBO'S "SECRET" INGREDIENT

Big Lisotte recalls: "Summers were wonderful in Biloxi, Mississippi. We spent every possible moment on the seawall out front, where we caught crabs and all kinds of fish. Sometimes at dusk, Pop would help us pull a two-man *seine* (net) to catch shrimp, crabs, and anything else that might appear. After dark we would walk the sandbar with a Coleman lantern and gig soft-shelled crabs and flounder—always on the lookout for the dangerous stingrays. Friday was always gumbo day. My grandmother insisted a fine big ham bone was essential to a great pot of gumbo. However, there were many Catholics in our group who were not supposed to eat meat on Friday. So Mama would secretly remove the big ham bone at the last minute, and everyone was happy."

Shrimp and Okra Gumbo

This recipe won first place at the American Heart Association Cookoff in January 1993.

1½ pounds fresh okra (frozen okra may be substituted; do not thaw.)
6 tablespoons oil, divided
1 tablespoon vinegar
4 tablespoons flour
2 cups onion, chopped
2 stalks celery, chopped
½ cup bell pepper, chopped
½ cup lean ham, diced (optional)
6 cloves garlic, minced
(1) 16-ounce can tomatoes, chopped
2 quarts seafood or chicken stock (or water)

2 bay leaves
½ teaspoon thyme, crushed
½ teaspoon cayenne pepper
1 tablespoon Worcestershire sauce
1 teaspoon liquid crab boil (optional)
2 pounds shrimp
1 pint oysters with liquid
½ cup parsley, chopped
½ cup green onions, chopped
Zest of 1 lemon
Salt and pepper

1. Wash and dry okra, remove stems, and slice in one-inch rounds. (If using frozen okra, do not wash.) Heat two tablespoons oil in a heavy saucepan other than black iron. Sauté okra in oil and vinegar, stirring often until ropiness is gone.

2. In another pot, make a dark roux with four tablespoons each of oil and flour. Add onion, celery, and bell pepper. Sauté until limp. Add diced ham, garlic, and tomatoes. Cook 10 minutes, stirring often. Add okra, stock, and seasonings. Cook 30 minutes.

3. Peel and devein shrimp, saving shells to boil for stock. Add shrimp and oysters to the soup. Return to a boil and cook five minutes.

4. Add parsley, green onions, lemon zest, and salt and pepper to taste. Serve over hot rice. Serves 8 to 10.

NOTE: It is best to freeze Shrimp and Okra Gumbo without the shrimp added. When you reheat, add fresh shrimp.

GUMBO

To Creoles and Cajuns, gumbo is the ultimate soup.

Gumbo can be made from whatever is on hand, but there are two kinds served most often in South Louisiana: seafood gumbo, usually made with okra—in fact, "gumbo" means okra in an African dialect—as well as crab, shrimp, and oysters; and turkey or chicken gumbo, made with andouille sausage.

Okra and filé powder are both thickening agents and can be used in both types of gumbo. Filé powder is made of ground sassafras leaves. It is added to gumbo for both its flavor and thickening powers. However, it breaks down if cooked for a long period. Always add it to the gumbo after the heat is turned off or at the table.

Gumbo is always served with rice, which is spooned into the bowls first. The gumbo is ladled on top. With a salad and French bread, gumbo makes a delicious meal.

Chicken and Andouille Filé Gumbo

It's a good idea to make this gumbo a day or two ahead because the flavor develops as it rests. If you're watching your fat intake, you can more easily remove it when it has congealed on top of the gumbo after the soup has been refrigerated.

Popcorn Rice is excellent with this gumbo.

1 fryer chicken, cut into pieces	Salt
3 tablespoons Paul Prudhomme's Poultry Magic	Cayenne pepper
½ cup oil	Thyme
½ cup flour	Bay leaves
2 cups onion, chopped	1½ pounds andouille sausage
½ cup bell pepper, chopped	(or any good smoked sausage)
2 stalks celery, chopped	Green onions, sliced
8 cups hot chicken stock	Parsley, chopped
(1) 16-ounce can tomatoes	Filé powder
3 cloves garlic, minced	

1. In a heavy Dutch oven, brown chicken that has been sprinkled with Paul Prudhomme's Poultry Magic in oil. Remove chicken and set aside. (Re-measure the oil to make sure you have ½ cup.) In the same pot, make a dark brown roux using the oil and flour.

2. Add onions and cook until they are translucent.

3. Add bell pepper and celery. Cook five minutes more.

4. Add hot stock, tomatoes, garlic, and seasonings to taste (except filé powder). Bring to a boil, and reduce heat to simmer. Add chicken and sausage. Simmer 1½ to 2 hours.

5. Adjust seasonings to taste and skim fat before serving. Serve over boiled rice. Garnish with green onion and parsley. Add filé powder at the table. Serves 8 to 10.

CREOLE VEGETABLE SOUP

The soup meat in this recipe can be boneless or bone-in. Bones add a wonderful flavor. However, most people prefer using boneless meat such as chuck. The extra stew meat in this recipe can be served as a dish itself. Serve with Creole Mustard or horseradish sauce.

This recipe makes a very thick vegetable soup. Add more water if desired. Serve with fresh corn bread.

5 to 6 pounds soup meat
(2) 1-pound cans tomatoes
4 onions, very coarsely chopped
5 carrots, very coarsely chopped
5 celery stalks, very coarsely chopped
²/₃ pound lima beans
1 pound snap beans
1 corn on the cob per person, cut into fourths
   (may substitute cut corn)

¹/₂ cup green onions, chopped
¹/₂ cup parsley, chopped
2 potatoes, quartered
1 tablespoon salt
2 teaspoons black pepper
Tabasco or other hot-pepper sauce to taste
¹/₂ teaspoon thyme
3 bay leaves
7 quarts water

1. In a 10-quart stockpot, place the beef, vegetables, and seasonings. Add the water and bring to a boil. Reduce heat to a simmer and partially cover. Skim off the scum that rises to the top. Simmer about four hours. Serves 10 to 12.

❖

HOT STUFF

There's something really hot in our Creole Delicacies Gourmet Shop just outside Cookin' Cajun Cooking School in The Riverwalk. A special section of our gourmet shop, known as the Heat Wave Room, offers some of the most fiery sauces around. The collection of hot sauces, many made in Louisiana, are guaranteed to heat up any dish. There's Bat's Brew and Vampire, both made "just down the road" from Translyvania, Louisiana. Cajun Rush is a salt-free hot sauce. And locally produced Mean Devil Woman hot sauce is made of vinegar, salt, garlic, onions, lime juice, and searing habañero peppers. The most blazing bottled pepper sauce is Dave's Insanity, a favorite among those who like their food flaming hot. If you find that a particular sauce sets your mouth on fire, don't drink gallons of water to put out the flames. Try a spoonful of sugar or a glass of milk to turn down the heat.

Oyster Artichoke Soup

We serve this wonderful soup at our Christmas parties, and everyone loves it. Serve with hot French bread to complement the rich flavor.

5 medium artichokes (or three 16-ounce cans artichoke hearts, drained)
1 tablespoon vinegar
Salt
¼ cup flour
¼ pound (1 stick) butter
1 tablespoon vegetable oil
1 cup onion, chopped
½ cup celery, chopped

1 bunch green onions, chopped
1 clove garlic, chopped
4 ounces lean ham, chopped
2 teaspoons parsley, chopped
1 quart turkey stock
1 tablespoon seasoned salt (or more, to taste)
1 teaspoon black pepper
5 dozen oysters with liquor

1. Boil fresh artichokes in salted water with vinegar 45 to 55 minutes, until tender. Drain and cool. Scrape leaves and chop hearts. Set aside.

2. In a large Dutch oven, brown flour in butter and oil for five minutes. Add onion, celery, and green onion. Sauté 15 minutes. Add garlic, ham, parsley, turkey stock, seasoned salt, pepper, artichoke scrapings, and hearts. Simmer 20 minutes.

3. In another pan, heat oysters and their liquor until edges curl. Drain off liquid into soup mixture.

4. Cut up oysters (or leave whole if small) and add to soup. Simmer 15 minutes more. Taste for seasoning. Serves 12.

Turtle Soup

Commander's Palace Restaurant's Turtle Soup is often mentioned as the very best, but every great restaurant in New Orleans serves its own version of this popular soup—all different, all delicious. Here is ours.

3 pounds boneless turtle meat
  (you may substitute veal)
1 cup oil
1 cup flour
1½ cups onion, chopped
1 cup celery, chopped
6 cloves garlic
(1) 8-ounce can tomato sauce (or 6 tablespoons
  tomato paste with ½ cup water)
2 quarts water
¼ cup beef extract
2 teaspoons celery salt

½ teaspoon cayenne pepper
4 bay leaves
2 lemons, halved
1 teaspoon thyme
¼ cup parsley, chopped
¼ cup fresh lemon juice

Garnish:
1 lemon, sliced thin
2 eggs, hard-boiled and chopped
Sherry

1. Cut turtle meat into cubes. Brown in hot oil. Lift out with slotted spoon and set aside.

2. In same oil, cook flour over medium heat until brown, stirring constantly. Add onion, celery, and garlic. Cook 10 minutes.

3. Add tomato sauce (or tomato paste with water), water, beef extract, celery salt, cayenne pepper, bay leaves, lemons, thyme, and parsley. Chop browned turtle meat very fine and add to pot. Simmer two hours. Add lemon juice. Check for seasoning; add salt if needed.

4. Serve in soup bowls. Garnish with egg and lemon slices. Pass sherry to be added as desired. Makes three quarts.

Big Easy Entrées

Though perhaps best known for their way with seafood, Cajun and Creole cooks use a variety of ingredients in their main courses.

It was not so long ago that most South Louisiana homes—at least the more rural ones—would have had their own supply of chickens and a few pigs. Chicken was a favorite in the area. Butchering a pig was traditionally a time of celebration, called a *boucherie.*

Duck is also a staple in the Bayou Country. Veal is found in the more sophisticated Creole dishes. Although Cajun and Creole chefs are not known for their beef dishes, you'll find several delicious beef recipes in this chapter that will surprise you. Cajuns and Creoles appreciate a good steak as much as anyone from Texas.

Fish and shellfish are the mainstay of South Louisiana entrees. Crabs, shrimp, crawfish, and oysters are enjoyed simply or as parts of more complicated dishes. Cajuns and Creoles are fortunate to have fresh fish available from both fresh- and saltwater. Many residents are avid fishermen, and families and friends often spend weekends at "fishing camps." Some of the best food in the world comes from the kitchens of those camps.

If you catch your own fish, gut them as soon as possible, and store them on ice or in a refrigerator. Use fresh fish within two days or freeze them immediately. If you buy your fish from a market, it's best to make your selections from whole fish and have filets trimmed to your specifications. Remember: good fresh fish should not have a "fishy" smell.

CHICKEN SAUCE PIQUANTE

We've discovered some foods are not best served immediately. The spices and flavors develop if the dish is allowed to rest for a while. Allow extra time for extra flavor when preparing these dishes. The extra flavor is worth it! Created by Lee Barnes.

8 chicken thighs, skin removed
1/4 cup oil
2 tablespoons butter
1 1/2 cups onions, finely chopped
1 cup celery, finely chopped
1 cup bell pepper, finely chopped
4 tablespoons flour
(1) 1-pound can tomatoes
1 heaping tablespoon tomato paste
4 cups hot chicken stock
4 cloves garlic, finely chopped

1 lemon, thinly sliced
1/2 teaspoon cayenne pepper
1/2 teaspoon black pepper
1 1/2 teaspoons salt
1 teaspoon basil
1 teaspoon thyme
1 teaspoon chili powder
4 bay leaves
1 cup green onion, finely chopped
1/2 cup parsley, finely chopped

1. Brown the chicken in oil in a heavy Dutch oven; remove and set aside.

2. Pour out all but two tablespoons of the oil. Add butter and, when hot, add the onions, celery, and bell pepper. Sauté slowly until the vegetables begin to change color and become transparent. Sprinkle in flour and mix well over low heat, stirring for about five minutes.

3. Add tomatoes and tomato paste, and cook five minutes longer. Then add the stock, stirring and mixing well. As the sauce simmers, add the garlic, lemon, cayenne, black pepper, salt, basil, thyme, chili powder, and bay leaves.

4. Simmer the sauce slowly for half an hour, and then add the chicken thighs. Cook until the chicken is tender; then add the green onions and parsley.

5. When the chicken is done, remove from the heat and let rest for half an hour. At this time, seasonings may be corrected. Serves 4 to 8.

LIL'S SMOTHERED CHICKEN

Lillian Lee, who once worked for us, still cooks the best red beans and fried chicken you'll ever eat. This is her recipe—or as close as we can make it—that we've passed on to others. It's one of the best versions of Chicken Sauce Piquante you'll ever taste.

5 pounds chicken, cut up, washed, and patted dry
Creole seasoning
3 tablespoons cooking oil or bacon drippings
1/3 cup flour
1 cup onion, chopped
1 cup celery, chopped
1 cup bell pepper, chopped
(1) 16-ounce can tomatoes

1/2 teaspoon basil
1/4 teaspoon white pepper
2 bay leaves
1 cup water
(1) 6-ounce can tomato paste
1/2 teaspoon thyme
1/4 teaspoon black pepper
Hot-pepper sauce to taste

1. Sprinkle chicken with Creole seasoning and brown in cooking oil. Remove and set aside.

2. Make a roux by heating oil or bacon fat in pot used to brown chicken. Add flour and stir constantly until flour is nut brown in color. Add onion, celery, and bell pepper. Cook until vegetables are soft.

3. Add remaining ingredients and mix well. Bring to a boil, and then reduce heat. Add chicken to sauce. Cover and cook 1 1/2 to 2 hours, or until chicken is tender. Serve with rice or pasta and toasted French bread. Serves 8 to 10.

ROAST TURKEY, CAJUN STYLE

Always choose the biggest turkey you can find because there are so many delicious ways to use what is left over.

TURKEY

(1) 20-to-24-pound turkey, thawed
Salt and pepper to taste
1 cup Good Garbage (see page 85)
¼ cup Worcestershire sauce
2 teaspoons dry mustard
¼ cup vegetable oil
¼ cup vinegar
1 tablespoon seasoned salt or poultry seasoning

1 tablespoon Bayou Magic Sausage Seasoning
(optional)
1 teaspoon black pepper
1 medium onion, chopped
3 ribs celery, chopped
4 bay leaves
½ bunch parsley stems, chopped
6 strips bacon

1. Remove neck and giblets from turkey; rinse well, sprinkle with salt and pepper, and place them in a saucepan with a quart of water containing Good Garbage (see page 85). Simmer over medium-low heat for two hours. Cool. Strain broth and save for making gravy. Pull meat from neck bones. Chop coarsely and save to add to dressing. The liver and gizzard may be chopped very fine and added to gravy and dressing.

2. Rinse thawed turkey under cold water. Drain. Place on a rack in a large baking pan. Mix Worcestershire sauce, dry mustard, oil, vinegar, seasoned salt or poultry seasoning, sausage seasoning, and black pepper. Spoon this mixture inside both cavities of the turkey; rub the rest all over the outside of the bird.

3. Fill both cavities with onions, celery, bay leaves, and parsley. Use skewers or strong toothpicks to secure skin on neck cavity. Use dental floss to truss the turkey cavities. Wrap lower part of each

drumstick with a piece of bacon. Arrange other strips of bacon across the breast of the turkey. Cover turkey loosely with aluminum foil. Roast in 325°F oven for approximately five hours.

4. Test by cutting open the area where the thigh joins the body of the turkey. (Use a flashlight to be certain of juice color. If no red or pink juices show, the turkey is done.)

5. Remove turkey from oven and allow it to rest for 15 minutes before carving. Remove turkey to carving board or platter. Pour all drippings from the baking pan into a large saucepan. When fat rises to the top, skim and remove. Conserve drippings for gravy.

GRAVY

¹/₂ cup (1 stick) butter or margarine
  (or substitute fat from turkey drippings)
¹/₂ cup flour
1 cup onion, chopped

Conserved turkey drippings
Conserved turkey stock, as needed to thin gravy
Conserved liver and gizzard, if desired
¹/₂ cup parsley, minced

1. In a large cast-iron skillet, melt butter or margarine. Add flour. Stir and cook over medium heat until light brown.

2. Add minced onion. Cook about five minutes, stirring often.

3. Add turkey drippings and stock; chopped liver and gizzard, if desired; and minced parsley. Simmer until ready to serve.

GAME-DAY TURKEY HASH

In New Orleans, New Year's Day means the Sugar Bowl, our Southeastern Conference bowl game. Turkey hash and grits were always served at the Beatties' lovely home on Exposition Boulevard facing Audubon Park.

At Cookin' Cajun, Turkey Hash continues to be a brunch favorite. You can substitute chicken if you prefer.

TURKEY HASH

1/4 pound (1 stick) butter
1/3 cup flour
2 cups onions, chopped
1/2 cup green onions, chopped
1/2 cup celery, chopped
1 cup parsley, chopped, and divided in half
(1) 8-ounce can mushroom pieces, drained
(or use fresh, sautéed mushrooms)
(1) 4-ounce jar or can pimento, sliced

3 bay leaves
6 cups hot turkey stock (see opposite page)
2 or more cups turkey meat
1 tablespoon seasoned salt
(Tony Chachere's is our favorite)
1 teaspoon Worcestershire sauce
1 tablespoon black pepper
1 teaspoon cayenne pepper
1/2 cup bell pepper, cut in small strips

1. Make a dark roux with butter and flour. Add onions. Cook five minutes, stirring often. Add green onions, celery, and half of the parsley. Cook 10 minutes.

2. Add mushrooms, pimento, and bay leaves. Gradually work in turkey stock. Then add turkey and seasonings. Cover and simmer 20 minutes. Add bell pepper strips and the rest of the parsley; taste for seasoning. Simmer five minutes longer.

3. Serve over hot grits with large pieces of corn bread. Turkey Hash is also excellent over noodles or mashed potatoes. Serves 12 to 15.

TURKEY STOCK

1 leftover turkey carcass with plenty of meat left on it (or cook a turkey from scratch)

1 cup Good Garbage (see page 85) or use chopped onion, celery, and parsley

1. Carefully remove all meat from the turkey. Shred meat coarsely with your fingers. Do not cube. Refrigerate until ready to use.

2. Put all bones, skin, and giblets in a large pot with water to cover. Add Good Garbage and bring to a boil. Reduce heat and simmer for two hours or so. Strain stock and set aside. When cool, skim fat from the top.

WILD DUCK IN RED WINE

This is a guaranteed, never-fail method from our friends Eddie and Becky.

4 wild ducks
1 can beef bouillon
1 can onion soup

1 can water chestnuts
(1) 8-ounce can mushroom pieces
1 cup red wine

1. Heat oven to 350°F. Place ducks, breast down, in a heavy Dutch oven. Mix next five ingredients and pour over ducks. Bake uncovered for two hours. Turn ducks breast sides up. Bake two hours longer. Serve with pan juices. Serves 4.

DIRTY RICE

Paw Paw hated the name Dirty Rice, but he loved this dish. Use it as a dressing with your turkey. It's also excellent as a stuffing for bell peppers or tomatoes.

8 ounces (1 cup) chicken livers, chopped (optional)
1 pound lean ground beef
1 pound bulk pork sausage (hot or mild) or turkey sausage
1/2 pound (1 stick) butter or margarine, divided in half
1 cup onion, chopped
1 cup celery, chopped
1 cup green bell pepper, chopped
2 cloves garlic, chopped

1 pound fresh mushrooms, sliced
1/2 teaspoon thyme
1/2 teaspoon basil
4 cups cooked rice
1 teaspoon salt
1 quart chicken stock, divided in half
1 teaspoon cayenne pepper
Salt to taste
1 bunch green onions, chopped
1 cup parsley, finely chopped

1. Sauté chicken livers, ground beef, and sausage in large Dutch oven until brown. Remove meat with a slotted spoon and drain on paper towels. Pour off most of the fat left in the pan. Add half the butter or margarine, onion, celery, bell pepper, and garlic to the Dutch oven. Cook until light brown, stirring often.

2. Wash, dry, and slice mushrooms. Melt remaining butter or margarine in a skillet until bubbly. Add mushrooms and sauté quickly over medium heat until brown. Add to onion mixture.

3. Add meat and seasonings.

4. Cook rice in one pint chicken stock plus water and salt as needed. Drain well. Add to meat mixture with green onions, parsley, remaining chicken stock, and salt to taste. Cover and bake in 400°F oven for 35 minutes. Serves 12.

Red Beans, New Orleans Style

Traditionally, Monday is Red Beans day in New Orleans. Almost every home and restaurant has a big pot of this local favorite simmering on the stove. Some like to add sausage to red beans while they cook. We prefer to panfry the sausage separately, then serve it on a plate alongside the Red Beans and Rice. Equally delicious is substituting pork chops, hamburgers, hot dogs, ham slices, fried chicken, and even breaded veal—as served at Mandina's Restaurant on Canal Street—for the sausage. Serve with hot French bread. Almost all of the men in our family like to put ketchup on their red beans. Red beans taste even better the day after they are cooked. They freeze well. Purée the leftover beans to make delicious bean soup.

3 pounds dried red kidney beans
   (Camellia brand if available)
8 quarts water
1 pound seasoning meat, such as ham or
   pickled meat, coarsely chopped
1 ham bone or ham hock

2 onions, chopped
3 ribs celery, chopped
3 cloves garlic, chopped (optional)
Salt and pepper to taste
1/4 pound (1 stick) butter (optional)

1. Sort beans to remove bad ones and stones. Rinse beans under cold water; do not soak. Put beans in a big pot with water. Add all other ingredients except butter. Bring to a boil over high heat. Reduce to medium high and allow beans to boil briskly for one hour longer, stirring often.

2. Reduce heat to medium low and continue to cook an additional hour. Check often to make sure beans are not sticking to the bottom of the pot. Mash beans against the side of the pot as you stir to break them down and make the mixture creamy. Add butter. Serves 12.

THE BOEUF GRAS It is another measure of our family's acknowledged love of food that every Mardi Gras our grandfather, known as Paw Paw, rode the Boeuf Gras float in the Carnival parade. Always the fourth float in the lineup, it depicts one of the oldest symbols of Carnival—the boeuf gras, or fatted calf. It represents the last meat eaten before the Lenten fast. It is traditional to eschew meat during the 40-day fast leading from Mardi Gras to Easter. The Boeuf Gras in the Mardi Gras Parade came to symbolize the meaning of the Carnival season.

COOKIN' CAJUN BEEF BRISKET

This recipe can be expanded to serve a crowd; serve at once or allow to cool in the refrigerator to be served the following day after the congealed excess fat from the pan gravy is removed and slicing is easier. Slice thinly across the grain for wonderful hot or cold sandwiches.

1 whole beef brisket (or two or three for a crowd)
(1) 4-ounce bottle liquid smoke flavoring
Celery salt
Black pepper

Garlic salt (optional)
(1) 13-ounce jar Woody's Cook-in Barbecue Sauce
*   Concentrate*

1. Put beef brisket in a glass dish or stainless-steel baking pan. Rub well with liquid smoke, celery salt, black pepper, and garlic salt. Cover tightly with aluminum foil. Refrigerate overnight.

2. The following day, without opening the foil, bake in a 275°F oven tightly covered for four hours. Uncover and pour Woody's sauce over the entire roast. Cover again; return to the oven for one hour. Serves 12.

Lemon-Pepper Beef Steaks

8 beef steaks (filets, ribeyes, T-bones or sirloins), cut 1¼-inches thick

8 tablespoons fresh lemon juice
Black pepper to taste (freshly ground is best)

1. Thirty minutes before cooking, rub steaks with lemon juice and black pepper. Allow to rest at room temperature.

2. Prepare barbecue grill with medium-to-hot fire, allowing coals to reach white stage. If using a gas grill, set temperature to medium hot. Place steaks on grill and cook five minutes on each side for rare, six minutes on each side for medium with the grill lid down. Turn steaks with spatula or tongs. Enjoy with hot French bread and plenty of butter. Serves 8.

Chaurice Sausage

This versatile sausage can be stuffed into casings or formed into patties. Fry the patties for breakfast, or crumble and use in jambalaya. Created by Lee Barnes.

$1^1/_2$ pounds lean pork
$^3/_4$ pound pork fat
1 cup onions, minced
$^1/_3$ cup parsley, minced
1 tablespoon garlic, minced
2 tablespoons hot green chilies, minced

2 teaspoons cayenne pepper
2 teaspoons black pepper
2 teaspoons thyme
$^1/_2$ teaspoon allspice
2 tablespoons salt
1 yard sausage casings

1. Put pork and fat through meat grinder. Add all other ingredients except casing. Mix well. Put through meat grinder again.

2. Stuff into casing. To cook, fry on low heat until done. Be sure to prick sausage well before frying to prevent rupturing. Yield: about 3 pounds.

GRILLADES

The secret of good grillades (pronounced "gree-ods") is making sure the meat is tender enough to cut with a fork. Try adding a little vinegar while the grillades are simmering to hasten the tenderizing process.

Grillades are served with grits. We recommend that you buy the old-fashioned slow-cooking grits or Quick Grits rather than the instant or microwave varieties. Their taste will invariably reflect the extra time it took to cook them.

We found we were always running out of the spice mixture included in this recipe, so we now make a double batch and suggest you do the same. It freezes well and will then be on hand when you're ready to use it.

This dish works well in a cast-iron Dutch oven.

1³/₄ pounds veal or beef round steak
Spice mixture:
   2 teaspoons salt
   1 teaspoon pepper
   ¹/₄ teaspoon cayenne
   5 cloves garlic, finely chopped
Flour
2 tablespoons unsalted butter

1 tablespoon oil
1¹/₂ cups onion, chopped
¹/₂ cup celery, chopped
¹/₂ cup bell pepper, chopped
(1) 1-pound can tomatoes
1¹/₄ cups beef stock
1 tablespoon vinegar (optional)

1. Trim all excess fat off steak. Cut into two-inch squares. Pound each square of meat with a meat tenderizer until each almost doubles in size. When about halfway through pounding each square, dip meat on both sides into the spice mixture, and then finish pounding. When completely finished pounding meat, rub each side with a little flour.

2. Fry the meat in the butter and oil. Add onions, celery, and bell pepper. Cook, stirring constantly, until the vegetables are tender. Add tomatoes, beef stock, and vinegar. Cover and simmer for about 30 minutes or until the meat is tender and a rich brown. Beef will require more cooking time than veal. Serve over hot grits. Serves 6.

SAUSAGE JAMBALAYA

Between New Orleans and Baton Rouge is a small town called Gonzales. It is known as the Jambalaya Capital of the World. Jambalaya is a great way to clean out the refrigerator. Thrifty Cajun and Creole cooks created Jambalaya to make a filling meal out of leftovers. We do the same.

We do not recommend using salt, pepper, or Tabasco in our Jambalaya because the meats are spicy enough. If you are substituting chicken or turkey, you may want to add the spices. If chaurice (hot sausage) is not available, Italian sausage works well. Tasso is a Cajun-spiced ham. To make your own Tasso, mix equal parts of white and red pepper. Pat this mixture on a ham steak. Grill or smoke the ham. You can cut the tasso into pieces and freeze it for later use. For Jambalaya, we suggest using converted rice. It holds up better. Try Jambalaya with shrimp or chicken.

½ pound chaurice (hot sausage)
¼ cup tasso
2 cups onion, chopped
1 bell pepper, chopped
2 stalks celery, chopped
3 bay leaves
½ teaspoon thyme
2 cups long-grain rice
(1) 1-pound can tomatoes, crushed, with liquid

3 cups hot chicken stock
4 cloves garlic, minced
1 pound andouille (smoked sausage), sliced
2 cups smoked ham, diced
4 green onions, sliced
¼ cup parsley, chopped
Salt to taste
Pepper to taste
Tabasco or other hot-pepper sauce to taste

1. Sauté hot sausage and tasso, in oil if necessary, for several minutes. In same oil or fat, cook onions thoroughly. Add bell pepper and celery. Cook until tender. Add bay leaves and thyme.

2. Add rice and stir until coated in the oil. Add tomatoes, chicken stock, garlic, sliced andouille, and ham. Bring mixture to a boil. Cover and let simmer about 30 minutes or until rice is done.

3. Just before serving, add green onion and parsley. Serve hot with toasted French bread and a green salad. Serves 8; or 10 ladies at a luncheon; or 4 hungry Cajuns! NOTE: If using Uncle Ben's Converted Rice, then use two cups rice, two cups stock, and one 16-ounce can tomatoes.

Mardi Gras Salad

This lively salad features the traditional Mardi Gras colors of purple for justice, green for faith, and gold for power.

1 head lettuce
1 cup purple cabbage, sliced

1 cup yellow bell pepper, sliced

1. Wash and dry lettuce. Tear into pieces. Place in large salad bowl.

2. Sprinkle cabbage and bell pepper on top. Pour one cup Creole Mustard Salad Dressing over salad. Toss and serve. Serves 12.

Creole Mustard Salad Dressing

2 tablespoons Creole Mustard
2 tablespoons vinegar (cane, red wine, or rice)
³/₄ cup oil

1. Blend mustard and vinegar. Slowly add oil; blend until smooth. Pour over salad.

48

CRAWFISH ÉTOUFFÉE

There's an old story about how crawfish came to Louisiana. When the Cajuns left Nova Scotia in 1755, the lobsters missed them so much that they decided to leave, too. They started swimming south, past Cape Hatteras, around the tip of Florida, past Alabama and Mississippi, until they finally found the Cajuns in the bayous of Louisiana. Their swim was so long and arduous that the beautiful, big lobsters shrunk—and that's how Louisiana got crawfish. These "little lobsters" liked the warmer but narrower waters of coastal Louisiana, so there they remain.

Shrimp can be substituted for crawfish in this recipe to make a tasty Shrimp Étouffée. Created by Lee Barnes.

1 cup onion, chopped
$^1/_2$ cup celery, chopped
$^1/_2$ cup bell pepper, chopped
3 tablespoons butter
3 tablespoons flour
2 tablespoons tomato paste
$1^1/_2$ cups crawfish tails, removed from shell

Fat from crawfish heads
2 cups crawfish stock or shrimp stock
$^1/_2$ cup green onions, chopped
$^1/_4$ cup parsley, finely chopped
1 teaspoon salt
$^1/_4$ teaspoon black pepper
$^1/_2$ teaspoon cayenne pepper

1. Sauté onions, celery, and bell pepper in butter. When limp, add the flour and stir for 10 minutes.
2. Add tomato paste and cook 10 minutes longer. Add the crawfish tails and fat. Cook for five minutes; then add stock.
3. Simmer covered for five minutes. Add the green onions, parsley, salt, black pepper, and cayenne pepper. Simmer 10 minutes more; then allow to rest for 20 minutes off the heat.
4. Reheat and serve over rice. Serves 4 to 6.

❖

MAKING CRAWFISH STOCK

Crawfish stock is made by boiling the heads and shells of the crawfish. Crack the claws, and boil all in three to four cups water. Add tops of green onions and allow to simmer 15 to 20 minutes.

Crawfish dishes can be as simple as boiled crawfish, hearty stews, and étouffées. Shrimp can be substituted for a slightly different flavor.

WHEN BOILING SEAFOOD

When dropped into boiling water, crabs tend to "throw off" their claws. If it is important to you that crabs keep their claws, chill them in the refrigerator a few hours before cooking. Boiled crabs and shrimp can be kept up to a week in the refrigerator. However, boiled crawfish are very perishable and should be eaten within two days.

CRAWFISH PIES

Go ahead and make the whole recipe; freeze the extra pies for those times when company drops in unexpectedly. It's like having money in the bank. Peeled and deveined shrimp may be substituted for crawfish tails. Recipe adapted by Susan Murphy.

1 cup butter	1 tablespoon seasoned salt
3/4 cup all-purpose flour	1 teaspoon ground black pepper
3 cups onion, chopped	1 teaspoon cayenne pepper
1 cup bell pepper, chopped	1 cup liquid coffee creamer
1 cup celery, chopped	1/2 cup brandy
1 teaspoon garlic, chopped	4 pounds crawfish tails, peeled
1 cup parsley, chopped	35 prepared individual pie shells, thawed
1 cup green onions, chopped	Seasoned bread crumbs and butter for topping
3 bay leaves	

1. In your largest Dutch oven, cook butter and flour until caramel colored. Add onions. Cook for five minutes over medium heat, stirring often. Add bell pepper, celery, garlic, parsley, green onions, and bay leaves. Cook 10 minutes, stirring often.

2. Add seasoned salt, pepper, coffee creamer, and brandy. Cook five minutes until mixture comes to a boil. Add crawfish tails and cook 10 minutes, allowing mixture to come to a low boil. Stir often. Remove from heat and take out bay leaves.

3. Preheat oven to 300°F. Place thawed pie shells on cookie sheet. Fill with crawfish mixture. Sprinkle seasoned bread crumbs and butter over all. Bake 20 minutes until light brown. Serves 35.

CRABMEAT RAVIGOTE

This rich crab dish is always one of our first choices as an appetizer at Antoine's Restaurant in New Orleans' French Quarter.

1 tablespoon onion, minced
1 tablespoon tarragon vinegar
1 tablespoon green bell pepper, minced
1 tablespoon pimento, minced
1 tablespoon anchovies, minced (or anchovy paste)

1 cup mayonnaise
1 pound lump crabmeat
2 cups lettuce, washed and shredded
Whole anchovies or strips of pimento for garnish

1. Cook onion and vinegar together in a microwave oven for 30 seconds on high. Mix in next four ingredients; chill.

2. Pick over crabmeat carefully to remove any pieces of shell. Gently mix crabmeat with sauce. Serve on a bed of shredded lettuce. Garnish with whole anchovies or strips of pimento. Serves 4.

Stuffed Crabs Snug Harbor

When using crabmeat in any dish, make sure you check it carefully for shell fragments.

¹/₃ loaf stale French bread
2 ounces Shrimp Essence (see pages 62, 85)
*   or crab stock, if available*
4 ounces milk
6 strips bacon
¹/₂ stick butter or margarine
1 medium onion, chopped
2 ribs celery, chopped
2 bay leaves

(1) 8-ounce can mushroom stems and pieces
¹/₈ teaspoon dried thyme, crushed
¹/₂ cup parsley, chopped
¹/₄ teaspoon cayenne pepper
Juice of ¹/₂ lemon
¹/₂ cup mayonnaise
1 pound crabmeat
¹/₂ cup seasoned bread crumbs

1. Toast bread lightly. Break it into pieces and put it in a bowl. Add shrimp or crab stock and milk. Stir and set aside.

2. In a large skillet, fry bacon until crisp. Crumble and set aside. Pour off most of bacon grease. Add butter, onions, celery, and bay leaves. Sauté over medium heat until wilted and almost brown. Add mushrooms with liquid, thyme, bread mixture, parsley, cayenne pepper, and lemon juice. Cook for 10 minutes, stirring often.

3. Remove from heat. Add mayonnaise, bacon, and crab meat. Stir gently until well mixed. Fill baking shells or ramekins with the mixture. Sprinkle tops with bread crumbs. Bake in a preheated oven at 300°F for 20 minutes. Serves 8.

BOILED CRABS

"Our Lake Pontchartrain blue-claw crabs are positively the best in the world," Big Lisette vows. "I have a license for ten crab traps on my pier. They keep me supplied with crabs all year long."

1 to 2 dozen live crabs
3 gallons boiling water

½ cup salt
¼ cup liquid crab boil (we prefer Zatarain's)

1. Fill bucket containing crabs with cold water to allow them to purge while you bring cooking water to a boil.

2. Add salt and crab boil to boiling water.

3. Using tongs, place crabs in the boiling water one at a time until all are in the pot. Cover and boil for 20 minutes.

4. Turn off heat. Let crabs rest in water for another 20 minutes. Drain, saving stock for gumbo if desired.

5. Allow crabs to cool at room temperature for two hours before refrigerating. Serves 4 to 6.

CRABMEAT REMICK

This is an elegant dish for dinner parties. It's adapted from a popular entrée on the Caribbean Room's menu at the famous Pontchartrain Hotel on St. Charles Avenue.

1 pound white crabmeat
1 cup mayonnaise
1/4 teaspoon celery salt
1/2 teaspoon dry mustard
1/4 teaspoon cayenne pepper

1/4 teaspoon Tabasco or other hot-pepper sauce
1/2 cup prepared chili sauce
1 teaspoon tarragon vinegar
4 strips bacon, cooked crisp

1. Pick over crabmeat carefully for shells; then place in four oven-proof ramekins.

2. Blend together other ingredients, except bacon, to form sauce. Gently stir one teaspoon of this mixture into the crab meat. Heat ramekins in 350°F oven until very warm. Place crisp bacon on top of each. Spread remainder of sauce on top. Place under the broiler until sauce bubbles and forms a glaze. Serve with toast points. Serves 4.

CRABMEAT MUSHROOM RICE

This dish is adapted from the Pontchartrain Hotel's famed Caribbean Room. However, it is very simple to make at home in a few minutes. Popcorn Rice is our preference in this dish.

6 large fresh mushrooms, sliced
2 tablespoons butter
1/2 medium onion, chopped
1 rib celery, chopped
2 tablespoons parsley, chopped

2 cups cooked rice
2 ounces Swiss cheese, diced
1 cup crabmeat, carefully picked for shells
1/2 teaspoon seafood seasoning

1. Sauté mushrooms in butter. Add onion, celery, and parsley. Cook for five minutes.

2. Add rice and Swiss cheese, stirring until the cheese is melted. Add crabmeat and seafood seasoning. Stir gently. Serve with toasted French bread. Serves 4.

CRAB CAKES LISETTE

1 pound crabmeat (white or claw meat)
2 to 3 slices bread
2 tablespoons milk
1 teaspoon seafood seasoning or celery salt
1 egg, beaten
1 tablespoon baking powder

1 tablespoon parsley, chopped
1 tablespoon onion, minced
1 teaspoon Worcestershire sauce
1 tablespoon mayonnaise
Oil for frying
Tartar sauce and lemon wedges for garnish

1. Always buy fresh crabmeat if available. If you must use frozen, thaw it overnight in the refrigerator. Carefully pick over crabmeat to remove any shell fragments. Set aside.

2. Tear bread into small pieces and put in mixing bowl with milk. Add other ingredients, except crabmeat, and mix well. Add crabmeat and mix gently. Shape in patties of desired size. Fry in hot oil until browned, turning once. Serve with chilled tartar sauce and lemon wedge. Serves 6.

TARTAR SAUCE

1 cup mayonnaise
1 large dill pickle, chopped
1 tablespoon parsley, chopped

1 teaspoon onion, minced (optional)
1 tablespoon olives stuffed with pimentos, chopped

1. Mix all ingredients. Chill. Serves 6.

STUFFED OYSTERS

1 pint oysters with liquor
1 cup green onions, chopped
1 cup onion, chopped
1/2 cup celery, chopped
2 tablespoons butter
1/2 cup parsley, chopped

2 hard-cooked eggs, mashed
8 plain crackers, crushed
1/2 teaspoon Tabasco or other hot-pepper sauce
Salt and pepper to taste
Butter and cracker crumbs for topping

1. Cut oysters into thirds, reserving liquor. Sauté green onions, onions, and celery in butter until soft. Add oysters and cook until their edges curl.

2. Add parsley, oyster liquor, eggs, and cracker crumbs. Cook to a moist consistency. Add Tabasco, salt, and pepper to taste.

3. Put in three or four baking shells or one casserole. Top with cracker crumbs and melted butter. Bake in 350°F oven for 20 minutes. Serves 3 to 4.

OYSTER EGGPLANT CASSEROLE

Created by Lee Barnes.

1 large eggplant	1/2 cup green onions, chopped
1 cup onion, chopped	1/2 cup light cream
4 tablespoons butter	1/2 teaspoon salt
1 cup bread crumbs	1/2 teaspoon black pepper
2 1/2 dozen oysters with liquor	3/4 cup cheddar cheese, grated

1. Pierce the eggplant several times and place it into a 350°F oven. Bake until tender, about 40 minutes. (If a fork plunges into the eggplant easily, it is done.) Allow to cool.

2. Sauté the onions in butter for 10 minutes, and then add the bread crumbs. Mix well. Remove from the heat and transfer mixture to a bowl. Simmer the oysters in their liquor with the green onions. Cook for about five minutes or until the edges of the oysters begin to curl.

3. Grease well a one-quart casserole. Peel and slice the eggplant into 1/4-inch slices; cover the bottom of the casserole dish with half the eggplant slices. Sprinkle about 1/3 of the onion-bread crumb mixture over the eggplant. Pour half the simmered oysters and their juices over the bread crumbs. Add the remainder of the eggplant, some more of the bread crumbs, and the remaining oysters. Sprinkle what's left of the bread crumbs over the top, then pour light cream, salt, and pepper over all.

4. Spread the grated cheese on top. Place the casserole dish in a preheated 350°F oven and bake for 15 to 20 minutes. Serves 6.

"Barbecued" Shrimp

We don't know how this popular shrimp dish got the name "barbecued" because it is oven-broiled or baked. For a quick version using a skillet on top of the stove, try La Don's Très Bien BBQ Shrimp Mix from our mail-order catalog.

3 pounds large fresh shrimp with heads,
*   if available*
1 tablespoon salt
2 teaspoons seafood seasoning
1 teaspoon ground thyme
3 tablespoons black pepper

3 bay leaves
1 clove garlic, minced (optional)
³/₄ pound (3 sticks) butter or margarine, melted
1 tablespoon olive oil
3 lemons, cut in half

1. Rinse shrimp under cold water and arrange in a large broiling pan. Mix together all seasonings and sprinkle over shrimp. Add garlic, if desired. Pour melted butter and olive oil over all. Squeeze lemons over all and put lemon rinds in pan.

2. Broil shrimp about seven inches from heat for seven to ten minutes on each side or until cooked. Do not overcook! Cooking time varies depending on the size of the shrimp. When you can see space between the shell and the meat, shrimp are done.

3. Serve in large soup bowls with the sauce from the pan spooned over shrimp. Provide plenty of hot French bread or hot corn bread for dipping in the sauce, and plenty of napkins. It is messy but delicious. Serves 6.

SHRIMP WRAPPED IN BACON

Years ago when shrimp were inexpensive and plentiful, we served these often. Now they are offered only on special occasions.

3 pounds jumbo shrimp
Seasoned salt and pepper to taste
1 to 2 pounds bacon, thinly sliced
1 cup barbecue sauce for dipping

1. Rinse shrimp under cold water. Peel and devein. (Boil shrimp shells for stock to use in other recipes.)

2. Sprinkle shrimp with seasoned salt and pepper. Wrap each shrimp with half a strip of bacon. Place in wire holder.

3. Grill over hot fire for three minutes on each side. Bacon may flare up at times. If so, lift off until flames subside, then replace over fire. Do not overcook or shrimp will be tough. Serve hot with barbecue sauce. Serves 12 as an appetizer; serves 6 as a main course.

Cajun Boiled Shrimp

We use what is known as the "dry boil method" to preserve the flavor.

10 pounds fresh shrimp, with heads if possible
1 large onion, quartered
4 ribs celery with tops, coarsely chopped
4 bay leaves
1 bunch parsley stems, chopped
$^1/_4$ teaspoon dried thyme
1 tablespoon salad oil

2 tablespoons vinegar
2 tablespoons seafood seasoning
2 tablespoons salt
2 tablespoons liquid crab boil
   (Zatarain's is our favorite)
2 tablespoons cayenne pepper (optional)

1. Preheat stove burner to medium-high heat.

2. Rinse shrimp under cold water and drain. Place shrimp in a heavy Dutch oven with all other ingredients. Mix well. DO NOT ADD ANY WATER. Cover tightly.

3. Place pot on preheated burner. Cook five minutes. Uncover and stir shrimp from bottom to top. Cover again and cook five more minutes. Stir again. By this point, the liquid from the shrimp should be boiling. Cover and cook for two to five minutes more until shrimp have turned pink and you can see space between the shrimp and its shell. Do not overcook.

4. Remove from heat. Let shrimp rest three minutes in the pot to absorb seasonings.

5. Drain, saving liquid to use in other recipes (we call this concentrated stock Shrimp Essence). Spread shrimp out on a platter or tray and allow them to cool. Serves 8 to 10.

GRILLED SHRIMP SKEWERS

1 pound raw shrimp, peeled and deveined
Creole seasoning to taste (Konriko Hot & Spicy
    preferred)

Garlic powder (optional)
1/8 pound (1/2 stick) butter, melted

1. Sprinkle shrimp with Creole seasoning and garlic powder. Skewer shrimp and place on a hot grill. Brush on butter and cook until done. Do not overcook! Serves 2.

REDFISH TREASURE ISLE

Lisette lives on Treasure Isle in Slidell, Louisiana, on Lake Pontchartrain. She catches redfish at night under lights on her pier.

1/4 pound plus 2 tablespoons (1 1/4 sticks)
*   margarine, divided*
1 teaspoon paprika
1/2 teaspoon thyme
1/2 teaspoon oregano
1 teaspoon garlic powder
1 teaspoon onion powder
1/4 teaspoon white pepper
1/4 teaspoon red pepper

1/4 teaspoon black pepper
2 tablespoons Worcestershire sauce
1 tablespoon lemon juice
6 redfish filets, 7 to 8 ounces each
*   (or substitute trout filets)*
1 pound lump crabmeat
1/2 pound Swiss cheese, grated
2 tablespoons parsley, chopped

1. Melt 1/4 stick margarine in a saucepan. Blend in all powdered seasonings. Stir in Worcestershire sauce and lemon juice. Dip fish filets into this mixture until both sides are well coated. Set aside.

2. In a large, heavy skillet melt, 3/4 stick margarine until a light smoke appears at about 400°F. Do not allow margarine to burn. Carefully place each fish filet in hot margarine, and cook for about two minutes on each side. If pan flares up, carefully remove from heat until flames subside, then resume cooking until fish is done. Set aside.

3. Pick over crabmeat to remove any shell. In a small skillet, sauté crabmeat in 1/4 stick margarine (we do not recommend using diet margarines that are largely water). Add grated cheese and parsley, lightly mixing until melted. Do not overcook.

4. Serve redfish topped with crabmeat mixture. Serves 6.

REDFISH COURT-BOUILLON

This famous Creole court-bouillon (pronounced "coo-be-yon") dish is served over rice, sometimes in a shallow bowl with lots of crusty, warm French bread. Created by Lee Barnes.

5 tablespoons flour
5 tablespoons butter or oil
2 cups onions, chopped
1 cup celery, chopped
³/4 cup bell pepper, chopped
3 cloves garlic, minced
3 cups canned tomatoes, drained
¹/2 small can tomato paste
1 cup fish stock (substitute bottled clam juice or
    Knorr Fish Bouillon)

1 cup dry red wine
¹/2 cup parsley, chopped
¹/2 cup green onions, chopped
1 teaspoon salt
4 bay leaves
¹/2 teaspoon thyme
2 tablespoons lemon juice
Tabasco to taste
2¹/2 pounds redfish fillets (other firm, fresh
    fish may be substituted)

1. Combine flour and oil or butter in a heavy Dutch oven. Cook, stirring constantly, about 10 minutes. Add onions, celery, bell pepper, and garlic. Cook about 10 minutes until brown, stirring occasionally.

2. Mix in tomatoes and tomato paste. Cook, stirring constantly, about five minutes. Add fish stock, wine, parsley, green onions, salt, bay leaves, thyme, lemon juice, and Tabasco. Simmer about 45 minutes.

3. Add fish. Simmer 10 to 15 minutes or until fish flakes when tested with a fork. Serve over rice. Serves 6 to 8.

Trout Meunière

Many recipes call for clarified butter, as does this one. To clarify butter, melt it over low heat. Do not brown. Strain melted butter through very fine cheesecloth. Created by Lee Barnes.

4 trout fillets	*Capers*
1/2 cup milk	*Worcestershire sauce*
Salt and pepper	*Lemon slices*
Flour to coat	*Parsley, minced*
1 1/2 sticks clarified butter, divided	

1. Soak fish in milk. Drain and pat dry. Season with salt and pepper. Coat with flour. Melt 1/4 cup butter in a heavy skillet. When hot, brown fillets on both sides. Remove to warm platter. Pour butter out of skillet.

2. Place remaining butter in skillet. When hot, add capers and Worcestershire sauce. Brown. Pour the mixture over fish fillets. Garnish with lemon slices and parsley. Serves 4.

Broiled Flounder with 1-2-3 Sauce

Hollandaise is a tasty topping for this dish.

FLOUNDER

4 flounders, cleaned and scaled	*Juice of 2 lemons*
1/4 pound (1 stick) butter, melted	

1. Score flounders across the top. Place in broiler pan with a little water. Pour melted butter and lemon juice over fish. Broil for 10 minutes for each 1/2-inch thickness of fish. DO NOT TURN. Allow to rest for five minutes before serving. Serve with 1-2-3 Sauce. Serves 4.

1-2-3 SAUCE

¼ *pound (1 stick) butter*
Juice of 2 lemons

(1) 5-ounce bottle Worcestershire sauce
½ *cup parsley, chopped*

1. Heat all ingredients in a small saucepan until mixture comes to a boil. Yield: 1½ cups sauce.

GRILLED SPECKLED TROUT LAFITTE

This dish is named for Louisiana's beloved pirate, Jean Lafitte.

12 medium trout filets
1 tablespoon seasoned salt
1 teaspoon black pepper
1 pound bacon, sliced
8 ounces (1 cup) almonds, slivered

½ *pound plus 2 tablespoons (2¼ sticks)*
  margarine, divided
*5 ounces (*½ *cup plus 2 tablespoons)*
  Worcestershire sauce
Juice of 3 lemons

1. Salt and pepper trout filets well. Wrap slices of bacon around each filet until covered from end to end. Place fish in a wire grilling basket; barbecue over hot coals. Allow bacon to flare up but not burn. Cook about three minutes on each side. Bacon will be cooked but not crisp. Remove from basket and arrange filets carefully on a deep platter to hold their juices.

2. In a small skillet, slowly sauté almonds in ¼ stick margarine until golden brown. Sprinkle almonds over fish filets.

3. In the same skillet, melt the remaining margarine. Stir in Worcestershire sauce and lemon juice. Bring to a slow boil. Pour over fish. Serve at once with hot French bread for dipping in sauce. Serves 6 to 8.

The Sweet Life

Cajuns and Creoles believe life is sweet, so you can imagine they're not ones to pass on dessert. We've included several traditional favorites, as well as some of our families' recipes that have proven popular in our Cookin' Cajun Cooking School classes.

Some traditional desserts have dramatic presentations, such as Cherries Jubilee or Bananas Foster, while bread pudding, for example, is homier. Fruit-flavored ice creams are also popular in our warm summer months. And generations of New Orleans children have grown up savoring icy snowballs—shaved ice saturated with sweetly flavored syrups.

Big Lisette remembers, "Summertime meant snowballs—and we loved them so! Also, homemade ice cream with all the mess and the trouble of ice, cream, salt, and hand cranking—and such delicious results!

"We also ate lots of fresh fruit in the summer. Gramps came home from the office each day by the Canal Streetcar and the Broad Bus. There was a fruit stand on the corner that he could not resist; he would arrive home with bags of beautiful peaches, pears, grapes, and plums.

"We often ate the Japanese plums off the tree in our yard, resulting in frequent stomach aches," she continues. "Almost every yard had a fig tree, and we all looked forward to homemade fig preserves. My grandmother taught me to 'put up' figs, peaches, pears, and strawberries—and we have used her recipes at Creole Delicacies Kitchens."

BANANAS FOSTER

This is our version of this very famous New Orleans dessert from Brennan's Restaurant, named for Richard Foster.

Be careful when flaming this dish. Though dramatic, it is not necessary. If you do choose to flame it, a copper chafing dish with a long wooden handle makes an authentic and romantic presentation. Reheat this delicious topping and serve over French toast, pancakes, or waffles.

5 bananas, on the green side
¹/₄ pound (1 stick) unsalted butter
1 cup dark brown sugar
¹/₂ teaspoon cinnamon (optional)

1 teaspoon vanilla
¹/₂ cup banana liqueur
¹/₂ cup rum
10 scoops vanilla ice cream

1. Quarter the bananas. Melt the butter in a skillet or frying pan. Add brown sugar and cinnamon, if desired, and cook over low heat, stirring until it becomes a thick paste. Add vanilla and banana liqueur; stir well. Cook about three minutes. Add banana slices and cook over medium heat, basting well with the sugar and butter mixture. Cook about five minutes. (Mixture will bubble while cooking.)

2. Heat the rum in a metal cup, ignite, and pour over bananas. (The rum will have a faint blue flame in the cup and will flame up when poured over the bananas.) Stir well to blend, then serve with pieces of bananas over vanilla ice cream.

NOTE: Ice cream is presented best if scooped into balls and frozen ahead of time. Allow one half banana per serving. Chill the serving bowls so ice cream balls and bowls are very cold when Bananas Foster is ready to serve. Serves 10.

BANANAS FOSTER WITHOUT ALCOHOL

If you want to make Bananas Foster without alcohol, use 5 bananas quartered and 2 sliced apples (leave skin on). Follow the regular recipe, but substitute 1 cup apple juice for the alcohol.

PECAN PRALINES

Traditionally, pralines were made with pecans because pecans are so plentiful in the South. Created by Lee Barnes.

1 cup dark brown sugar	*2 tablespoons butter*
1 cup white sugar	*¼ teaspoon vanilla*
½ cup evaporated milk	*1 cup pecan halves*

1. Combine sugar and milk, and bring to a boil, stirring occasionally. Add butter, vanilla, and pecans. Cook until the syrup reaches the "soft ball stage"—238°F. Cool for five minutes; then beat with a wooden spoon until the mixture starts to thicken.

2. Drop by tablespoons onto a well-greased flat surface (aluminum foil works well). The candy will flatten out into large cakes about three to four inches in diameter. When candy cools, store in an airtight container. Yield: 20 pralines.

PECAN PRALINES

Legend has it that in the 1600s, Marshal Duplesis-Preslin's cook invented the praline in France. These first pralines were made with almonds. When the French came to New Orleans, they remembered this candy and made it with our delicious pecans that grew wild. Millions of these candies have been exported from New Orleans to destinations around the globe.

Famous New Orleans Pecan Pie

We suggest prebaking the pie shell or tart shells for about seven minutes at 350° F. For best results, use weights in the pie shell. Some of our favorite variations of this recipe follow.

3 extra large eggs
1 cup brown sugar, packed
1 cup corn syrup, dark or light

1 teaspoon vanilla
1 cup pecans, coarsely chopped or halved
$^1/_8$ teaspoon salt

1. Beat eggs until frothy. Add other ingredients, mix well, and bake in a preheated 350°F oven for 40 to 45 minutes. Yield: (1) 9-inch pie.

VARIATIONS:

PECAN PIE TARTS

3 extra large eggs
1 cup brown sugar, packed
1 cup corn syrup, light or dark

1 teaspoon vanilla
2 cups pecans, coarsely chopped
$^1/_8$ teaspoon salt

1. Prepare using same methods as Famous New Orleans Pecan Pie. Create your own, or purchase packaged tart shells. Yield: 16 tarts.

BOURBON PECAN PIE

Add one tablespoon bourbon whiskey to the filling before baking.

CHOCOLATE PECAN PIE

After prebaking the pie or tart shells, sprinkle them with chocolate pieces. Then pour in pie filling.

CREAM CHEESE PECAN PIE

Soften eight ounces cream cheese. Mix with $1/4$ cup powdered sugar and one egg or liquid-egg substitute. Spread over pie or tart shell, and pour in filling.

ALMOND PIE

Substitute sliced or slivered almonds for pecans. Use almond extract instead of vanilla.

BREAD PUDDING WITH AMARETTO SAUCE

Nearly every restaurant has its own version of this great New Orleans recipe. We believe this one created by Lee Barnes to be truly the best.

The best bread puddings were created by chefs who experimented with the traditional recipe. Any fresh fruit, or canned fruit with its syrup, or dried fruit can be used. Try orange slices with a little Grand Marnier, apples, raisins, or cinnamon and nuts—particularly good for holiday entertaining. Use your imagination and any ingredients in season. Leftover bread pudding makes a wonderful breakfast. Warm it in the microwave and enjoy it with a good cup of coffee and chicory.

(1) 10-ounce loaf stale French bread
1 quart milk (if bread is very hard, you'll probably
   need more milk.)
¹/₂ cup sugar

1 cup raisins
1 tablespoon vanilla
6 eggs

BREAD PUDDING

1. In a large bowl, soak bread in milk. Add sugar, raisins, and vanilla. Add eggs. Mix very lightly. Place in a well-buttered baking dish.

2. Bake at 375°F for 30 to 45 minutes. Remove from oven. While hot, poke holes in cake with the end of a wooden spoon. Splash with Amaretto liqueur. Pour hot Amaretto Sauce over bread pudding to penetrate the pudding as well as glaze the top. Serves 12.

AMARETTO SAUCE

¹/₄ pound (1 stick) unsalted butter
1 cup powdered sugar

¹/₄ cup Amaretto liqueur

1. Over low heat, melt butter, add sugar, stirring constantly. Add Amaretto. Heat slowly for one or two minutes.

Praline Sauce

Toasted pecans give this delicious sauce its flavor. Toast pecans in a dry skillet or bake in a 350° F oven for a few minutes. Once they cool, the pecans become crunchy and develop an unparalleled flavor.

Serve Praline Sauce over ice cream, cheesecake, or pound cake. It should be stored in the refrigerator. For a true taste of the South, try Praline Sauce on waffles, French toast, pancakes, or biscuits. Store in a decorative jar to enjoy or give as a gift.

2 cups white corn syrup
2 cups dark corn syrup
2 cups pecan halves or pieces, toasted
1/2 cup cane syrup

1/2 cup sugar
1/2 cup water
1 teaspoon vanilla

1. Combine dark and light corn syrup, pecans, cane syrup, sugar, and water in a saucepan; heat to dissolve sugar. Remove from the heat and cool. Add vanilla. Yield: about 7 cups.

UNFORGETTABLE FRUIT CAKE

This is our grandmother's treasured recipe, which she always made two weeks before Christmas.

1 pound (4 sticks) butter
1 pound (2²/₃ cups) sugar
10 eggs
1 teaspoon ground nutmeg
1 teaspoon ground cloves
1 pound (2²/₃ cups) flour
4 heaping teaspoons baking powder
1 pound (2²/₃ cups) raisins
1 pound (2²/₃ cups) currants
1 pound (2²/₃ cups) pitted dates, chopped

1 pound (2²/₃ cups) citron, cut up
½ pound (1¹/₃ cup) candied lemon peel, sliced thin
½ pound (1¹/₃ cup) candied orange peel, sliced thin
1 pound (2²/₃ cups) pecan pieces
1 pint (2 cups) maraschino cherries with juice
(1) 16-ounce can crushed pineapple with juice
1 pint (2 cups) Fig Preserves with juice

1 pint (2 cups) bourbon whiskey

1. Prepare many different sizes of baking tins a day ahead. Grease tins well with butter. The original recipe called for lard but Maw Maw always used butter. Cut two pieces of heavy brown paper to fit each tin. Butter the paper and place in tins.

2. Cream butter and sugar. Add two eggs at a time, mixing well. Mix together nutmeg, cinnamon, and cloves; add slowly to egg mixture.

3. Mix baking powder and flour. Sift together. In another bowl, put pecans and all fruit except cherries, pineapple, and figs. Sift flour-baking powder mixture over fruit. Mix with your hands. Add egg mixture to fruit mixture. Add cherries, pineapple, and Fig Preserves.

4. Pour batter into prepared tins. Place in preheated 200°F oven for two or more hours. Do not disturb except to test cakes after 1½ hours with a toothpick or straw. Cakes should be a little moist when done, not dry.

5. When cool, make holes in each cake with an ice pick or toothpick. To keep cakes moist, pour two ounces of bourbon whiskey (apple or cherry juice may be substituted) on each cake. Repeat this about once a week until cakes are eaten. Yield: 15 pounds of various-sized cakes.

NOTE: Alcohol preserves these cakes at room temperature. We recommend refrigeration of cakes if apple or cherry juice is substituted for the bourbon whiskey.

Mississippi Mud Cake

Forget about that diet and dive in. It's worth it!

BATTER

1/2 pound (2 sticks) butter
4 eggs
2 cups sugar
1/3 cup cocoa

1 1/4 cups flour
1 cup pecans, chopped
1 teaspoon vanilla
3 cups mini-marshmallows, divided

1. Cream butter. Add eggs and beat well. Add sugar, cocoa, flour, pecans, vanilla, and 1 1/2 cups marshmallows. Mix well.

2. Pour into buttered 9 x 13-inch dish or pan. Bake in a preheated 350°F oven for 30 to 35 minutes. Remove from oven, and sprinkle the remaining 1 1/2 cups marshmallows over the top of the hot cake.

ICING

1/4 cup (1/2 stick) butter, melted
1 pound confectioners' sugar
1/3 cup cocoa

1/2 cup evaporated milk
1 cup pecans, chopped

1. Mix together all ingredients and spread over warm cake. Cool before cutting into squares. Yield: 30 to 40 servings.

PECAN CREAM CHEESE PIE

You'll need two mixing bowls to prepare this recipe. Created by Lee Barnes.

8 ounces cream cheese, softened to room
   temperature
4 eggs
6 tablespoons sugar, divided

2 teaspoons vanilla, divided in half
3/4 cup corn syrup
4 ounces (1/2 cup) pecans, chopped
9-inch pastry shell

1. Put the softened cream cheese in a mixing bowl. Add one egg, 4 tablespoons sugar, and 1 teaspoon vanilla. Continue beating until the mixture is well creamed. Set aside.

2. In a separate mixing bowl, place three eggs, 2 tablespoons sugar, corn syrup, and remaining vanilla. Beat until well blended.

3. Pour cream cheese mixture into a nine-inch pastry shell. Level it off, then spread with chopped pecans. Stir the corn syrup mixture well; carefully pour the mixture over the chopped pecans. Bake in a preheated 375°F degree oven for 35 minutes. Yield: (1) 9-inch pie. Serves 8.

HEATH BAR CHEESECAKE

Created by Susan Murphy. We all beg her to make this wonderful dessert.

CHEESECAKE BATTER

(3) 8-ounce packages cream cheese
(3) 8-ounce containers sour cream
³/₄ cup sugar

3 eggs
2 teaspoons vanilla
3 tablespoons unsalted butter, melted

CRUST

1¹/₂ cups graham crackers, ground
3 Heath candy bars

¹/₄ cup sugar
6 tablespoons unsalted butter, melted

1. Soften cream cheese (microwave low.) Blend in sour cream and sugar. Add eggs one at a time, beating well. Add vanilla and butter. Beat well.

2. Grind graham crackers in food processor. Measure again to be sure you have 1¹/₂ cups crumbs. To crumbs in food processor, add two Heath bars broken into pieces, sugar, and butter. Grind together.

3. Spray a nine-inch springform pan with nonstick baking spray. Press crumb mixture on bottom. Chop the third Heath bar coarsely and sprinkle over crumb mix. Press down.

4. Preheat oven to 325°F. Bake crust seven minutes. Pour cheesecake mixture onto crust and bake at 325°F for 45 minutes until set. Turn off oven and let cake remain in oven 15 minutes. Cool. Refrigerate overnight or at least four hours before serving.

SERVING VARIATION: Spread sour cream over the cheesecake. Top with your favorite fruit. Dental floss works great to cut a cheesecake! Serves 16.

LAGNIAPPE

In Louisiana, *Lagniappe* (pronounced "lan-yap") means "a little something extra." The following recipes are little extras that we use in Cookin' Cajun Cooking School classes. They can make the difference between a good meal and a great one.

PEPPER VINEGAR

Long before the recent craze for flavored vinegars became a hit, Cajun and Creole cooks were adding a little zest to various dishes with Pepper Vinegar.

Bird or other small, hot peppers | *Cider or red wine vinegar*

1. Wash peppers and drain them. Pack into a narrow-necked bottle.

2. Fill with vinegar and tightly cap the bottle. Allow to stand at room temperature for several days to achieve full flavor.

PEPPER SHERRY

Pepper Sherry is made the same way as Pepper Vinegar; subtitute sherry for vinegar.

Use this flavored sherry to pep up turtle soup, turnips or other greens, stews, and bean soups.

Muffuletta Italian Sandwich or "Mini" Muffulettas

Part of New Orleans' Italian heritage, Muffulettas are offered by almost every area caterer. These sandwiches are very popular with all ages. True Muffuletta bread is 10 inches in diameter with sesame seeds on top. You can use most any Italian loaf.

2 round Muffuletta loaves of bread or 20 to 30
    mini buns
(1) 8-ounce jar olive salad (we recommend
      Progress Grocery Olive Salad)

$\frac{1}{2}$ pound Italian salami, thinly sliced
$\frac{1}{2}$ pound Provolone cheese, thinly sliced
1 pound Italian ham, thinly sliced

1. Slice bread across. Arrange layers of olive salad, salami, cheese, and ham.

2. Cut sandwiches in half or in quarters. Though some chefs serve them cold, we like to warm them in the oven until the cheese has melted. Serves 2 hungry people as a main course.

CITRUS MARMALADE

A treasured Christmas gift from our friend Red.

12 oranges
2 grapefruits
3 lemons

1 cup water
Sugar to measure
2 teaspoons almond extract

1. Wash fruit well. Squeeze juice from fruit and set aside.

2. Place fruit skins in pressure cooker. Add one cup water. Cook at 15 pounds pressure until the signal jiggles. Drain liquid from cooker and add it to reserved juice.

3. With a teaspoon, scrape white pulp from skins and remove stems. Coarsely grind skins in meat grinder or food processor; add to juice.

4. Add one measure of sugar to each measure of juice and peel. Bring to a boil. Reduce heat to simmer; stir often.

5. When mixture thickens, remove from heat and stir in almond extract. Pack in sterile jars and seal. Yield: 6 half-pint jars.

DEFINITIONS

BEIGNET: a light, square doughnut usually dusted with powdered sugar.

CAJUN COOKING: robust "country" food featuring one-pot meals using homegrown vegetables, peppers, spices, and wild game (raccoon, opossum, turkey, rabbit, turtle, seafood).

CAJUNS: Louisiana residents descended from French settlers of Nova Scotia who moved south to escape the English, settling in the rich bayou country of South Louisiana.

CRAB AND SHRIMP BOIL: a local product used to season boiled seafood; available in dry or liquid form.

CREOLE COOKING: usually highly seasoned food featuring rich sauces, rice, tomatoes, okra, peppers, and seafood; refined "city" food.

CREOLES: descendants of early French and Spanish settlers who brought West Indies and other cooking influences to the New Orleans area.

CREOLE TOMATOES: highly prized tomatoes, grown locally in rich Mississippi River delta soil; incredible flavor and texture.

DRY BOIL SHRIMP: our method of cooking shrimp to retain maximum flavor, using "good garbage" and crab boil but no added water.

ÉTOUFFÉE: a dish such as shrimp or chicken cooked slowly in a covered pot with vegetables and seasonings; smothered; stewed.

FILÉ POWDER: dried, ground sassafras leaves used to thicken gumbo and add unique flavor.

GOOD GARBAGE: scraps and trimmings from onions, celery, carrots, garlic, and parsley, saved in the freezer, and then mixed with black peppercorns and two or three bay leaves to make stock or to season boiled seafood. Bitter vegetables (cabbage, cauliflower, broccoli, turnips, brussel sprouts) add an undesirably strong flavor to stock.

HERBSAINT, OR *LIQUEUR D'ANIS*: "The Spirit of New Orleans" as served in the Old Absinthe House, a famous New Orleans landmark; used in Oysters Rockefeller Sauce.

MEUNIÈRE: a popular butter sauce used on seafood.

NEW ORLEANS: otherwise known as "Big Easy," "Crescent City" (referring to the sharp bend in the Mississippi River on which it lies), and "The City That Care Forgot."

POPCORN RICE: a special type of rice grown in southwest Louisiana that has a nutty flavor and smells like popcorn while cooking.

ROUX: a cooked mixture of equal parts of fat and flour used as the base of many Cajun and Creole dishes.

SHRIMP ESSENCE: the spicy concentrated shrimp broth resulting from the dry boil method.

ZEST: a thin outer skin of an orange or lemon used as flavoring.

INDEX